Praise for *Stronger than Steel*

"Make no mistake: St. Thérèse of Lisieux, the Little Flower, is indeed much *stronger than steel.* France entered WWI in 1914. Although St. Thérèse had passed away 17 years before, she was vividly there in battle in the midst of the French troops. After the war, soldiers flooded the Carmel in Lisieux with letters about how this once-cloistered nun protected them, renewed their faith, saved them, even appeared to them, taking some by the hand amid the bullets and bloodshed. Each letter is a treasure, a true account of God's presence in the darkness. If there is any book that will bring you hope in these unsettling times and a quiet joy burrowing to the depths of your soul, look no further. Thank you, Fr. Longenecker, for bringing this treasure to us. St. Thérèse, pray for us!"—SISTER MARY NORBERT of the Norbertine Canonesses of the Bethlehem Priory of St. Joseph

"In the years after the death of the young nun Thérèse Martin an avalanche of letters from around the world descended on the convent in Lisieux recounting the miracles and answers to prayer given by the saint. This collection of letters from soldiers fighting in the First World War is truly astonishing, moving, and inspiring. I wholeheartedly recommend this book to renew your faith in Christ, your devotion to the saints, and your conviction that God answers prayer and works miracles in the world today."—DAN BURKE, President, Avila Foundation

"Saint Thérèse is very well known by her fruits, but we don't know the half of them. For those who think of her as limiting herself to the religious life, this book will be a revelation. It shows her weakness in mortal life translated into glorious power on the battlefield, her illness translated into miraculous healing, and her death translated into protection from death. Multiple soldiers present to her their *Croix de Guerre* for she was there for them on the battlefield: appearing to them in the sky, kneeling in compassion before them, leading them to safety. All of this is told with the innocent directness of the young warriors themselves. These letters are a testimony to the truth of the promise of the Lord Jesus that the one who abided in Him would bear much fruit. Thérèse did both, and we are still learning how much."—FR. LUKE BELL, author of *Staying Tender: Contemplation, Pathway to Compassion*

"St Thérèse is often wrongly presented as a dainty, sentimental saint, not the sort to appeal to fighting men facing imminent violent death. But these touching letters from French soldiers show how much affection they had for Thérèse and, if their reports are to be believed, just how much affection she lavished on them in return from Heaven. This fascinating collection of letters amounts to a practical exposition of the doctrine of the Communion of Saints. It will surely instill readers with even more confidence in the intercessory power of the saint of Lisieux."—PATRICK KENNY, editor of *To Raise the Fallen: The War Letters, Prayers, and Spiritual Writings of Fr. Willie Doyle, S.J.*

"Once upon a time, I harbored a distaste for the widespread devotion to St. Thérèse of Lisieux. I found it sentimental, cloying, excessively cute. I imagine quite a few Catholics (and others) felt the same way. *Stronger than Steel* is the ultimate antidote to this misconception. These letters from the Front will convince all but the most skeptical that the Little Flower *was* present in the mud, blood, and chaos of the trenches; not only bringing spiritual consolation to the soldiers, but protecting many of them from shells and bullets. This a book to deepen your faith in supernatural realities."—MAOLSHEACHLANN Ó CEALLAIGH, author of *Inspiration from the Saints: Stories from the Lives of Catholic Holy Men and Women*

STRONGER THAN STEEL

Lourdes le 20 Mars 1919

Monsieur Cazaubon Emile ex sergent du 4ème Régiment
de Zouaves 11e Cie Secteur postal 131, actuellement
11 Rte de barbes à Lourdes. Htes Pyrénées.

Ma très Révérende Mère,

J'ai l'honneur de vous adresser
un petit compte rendu des grâces que j'ai obtenues de
Sœur Thérèse de l'enfant jésus. Au début de la
guerre le 2 août 1914 je ne la connaissais pas encore, ce ne
seulement dans le courant de l'année 1915, par l'intermé-
diaire de ma femme, elle me donnait une médaille.
Que j'attachais à ma chaîne de montre, et que je porte depuis
cette date là fièrement sur ma poitrine. Et depuis ce jour je me
mis sous sa protection, je l'ai souvent implorée et principalement
pendant les Batailles de Verdun, et de la Somme, je lui
demandais de me donner du courage, et de me protéger.
Le 21 Mars 1918 lorsque la grande
offensive Allemande se déclanchait j'appartenais au 4ème
Régiment de Zouaves, je la priai beaucoup, la situation était
critique, le 25 Mars le Régiment en alerte et nous voilà bientôt
engagé dans le grand combat. Le 28 à 15h 50 nous recevons
l'ordre d'attaquer le Village de Boulogne la Grasse (Oise)
et pour arrêter l'avance des Allemands. Il était

STRONGER THAN STEEL

Soldiers of the Great War
Write to
Thérèse of Lisieux

Translated by
Sr Marie de l'Enfant Jésus
(Sr. Marie of the Child Jesus)

Foreword by
Fr. Dwight Longenecker

Angelico Press

Originally published in French as
Nous les poilus, Plus forte que l'acier,
Lettres des tranchées à Thérèse de Lisieux
© Les Éditions du Cerf, 2014
24, rue des Tanneries, 75013 Paris, France

First published in English by Angelico Press, 2021
English translation by
Sr. Marie of the Child Jesus © 2021
Foreword © Fr. Dwight Longenecker, 2021

For information, address:
Angelico Press
169 Monitor St.
Brooklyn, NY 11222
www.angelicopress.com

pbk: 978-1-62138-718-3
cloth: 978-1-62138-719-0
ebook: 978-1-62138-720-6

Cover design: Michael Schrauzer
Cover images and frontispiece
© Archives du Carmel de Lisieux

Foreword

by Fr. Dwight Longenecker

Here in the American South there is a term for a feisty but feminine woman. She is called a "steel magnolia." St Thérèse of Lisieux is often nicknamed "the Little Flower" but once one gets to know her one realizes that if she is a "Little Flower," she is a steel magnolia. She's tender but she's also tough. She's devout and she's determined.

One of the most famous photographs of Thérèse shows her dressed in armor as St Joan of Arc. It was an apt role for her to play in the quaint little drama in the convent. This steel magnolia was a spiritual warrior. She wrote, "Sanctity! It must be won at the point of a sword!" And during her final illness she cried out, "I will die with my weapons in my hands!"

The theme of spiritual warfare is a constant in the Christian life. From the great sagas of the Old Testament through to the militant language in the Psalms and St Paul exhorting us to "put on the whole armor of God," we are encouraged to see the spiritual life as a battleground and ourselves as "soldiers of Christ."

While we "do not fight against flesh and blood, but against principalities and powers," it is true that down through history there have been times when the powers of darkness have assumed visible form and presented as tyrants with fully armed military cohorts, secret police and all the instruments of worldly power. At such times those who "fight the good fight" are called to also take up arms.

A Christian is a person of peace, and one never goes to war lightly or rashly. However, when the prevailing evil is clear and present, the Christian is reminded that "all it takes for evil to triumph is for enough good men to do nothing." In the major conflicts of the twentieth century the powers of antichrist presented their faces unmasked. When the evil was clearly marauding across the world, those who stood for Christian values had to do battle not only in the spiritual but also in the physical realm.

In the First World War, Germany (allied with the Turks, Austria and Italy) marched against France (allied with Russia, Britain and the USA). The fighting was the most bitter and deadly the world had ever seen. The suffering of the young men in the trenches was heartbreaking and relentless.

Thérèse Martin had died in 1897, just seventeen years before war broke out. In those years her book *The Story of a Soul* had been published and her fame had begun to spread. The book was hugely popular and quickly moved not only around France, but around the world through the French colonies in Africa and Indochina. Along with the growing devotion to Thérèse was an increasing call for her canonization. To this end the faithful from around the world wrote to the Mother Superior at the Carmelite convent bearing witness to the miracles and personal encounters they had had from the Little Flower.

Pope Pius X opened the cause for Thérèse's canonization in 1914, the same year the war broke out. This remarkable collection of letters from French soldiers fighting in the Great War is an abiding sign of the little saint's supernatural powers. She said on her deathbed, "I will spend my heaven doing good on earth," and she wasted no time! These letters from brave young soldiers tell how she appeared to them, how she miraculously protected them, delivered them from danger, healed them and encouraged them in battle.

In reading these astonishing and moving testimonies I am reminded of my own encounter with St Thérèse. In the summer of 1987 I was a young Anglican minister who had just completed his first assignment. I had three months free before my next post commenced, so I decided to make a pilgrimage to Jerusalem—hitchhiking from England and staying in monasteries en route.

The first leg of my journey was the ferry crossing to France. I got a late start and unfortunately missed the ferry sailing from Portsmouth on the south coast of England to the French port of Cherbourg in Normandy. I had planned to travel from there to the monastery of Mont St Michel. However, having missed the boat, I took the next available crossing, which was to Le Havre—further East along the Normandy coast. Getting off the ferry midafternoon, I had the task of finding a place to stay for the night. Looking at the map I noticed that the town of Lisieux was on my path. I had heard of St Thérèse of Lisieux and reckoned there might be some sort of hostel for pilgrims in the town.

I was right. On arrival I spotted "L'Hermitage"—a large hostel right next to the Carmelite convent in the middle of Lisieux. I entered and asked the young nun at the desk if I might have a room for the night as I was on pilgrimage. She smiled and showed me to a pleasant room, spartan in its monastic furnishings. After a stroll up the hill to the basilica dedicated to Thérèse and supper in the shared dining room, I headed up to my room and conked out. It had been a long and adventurous first day of my trek to Jerusalem.

I opened the shutters on the tall window of my room which overlooked the convent where Thérèse lived and died. It was a balmy summer evening and the breeze wafted the gauze curtains lightly as I went to sleep. About three o'clock in the morning I woke up, alert and conscious of what I can only describe as a strong, benevolent female presence in the room. I sat bolt upright aware and in tune with this revenant. I felt it was Thérèse.

Remember, I was an Anglican priest at the time, from a strongly Evangelical, Protestant background. We were not inclined to believe in the intercession of saints, and we were *certainly* not inclined toward the appearance or presence of saints—having been taught that Catholics "prayed to dead people." Such "traditions of men," we were told, were akin to necromancy and thus forbidden.

But during my Anglican training I had become much more open-minded about things Catholic and guessed that the presence in the room might very well be that of the young French woman.

After about fifteen minutes I went back to sleep, but the next day I visited the Carmelite convent and the Martin family home *Les Buissonnets*—where I purchased an English translation of *The Story of a Soul.* I clearly remember setting out on the road from Lisieux to Caen with my thumb out saying to Thérèse, "I have read that you pray for priests. Even though I am not a full member of your family I ask that you pray for me."

I am convinced that she did just that and protected me and traveled with me on my great adventure that summer, and that furthermore, she has been with me in the greater adventure ever since. How is it that eventually I would become not only a full member of her family, but one of her priests—even though a married man? I have no doubt it has been due to the intercession and protection of *ma petite sœur*—my little sister—the steel magnolia.

My experience on that summer night fits harmoniously with the testimonies of the young French soldiers collected here. As you read them be reminded that we are all called to the Great War—the spiritual war—and that this valiant soul (whom Pope Pius X called "the greatest saint of modern times") never fails to encourage and assist us in battle.

Preface

The 1914–1918 deluge of fire and iron didn't fail to arouse a call to faith and an aspiration to miracles. It is significant that the *Poilus*[1] in the trenches didn't invoke a male but a female saint, and, among all the female protectresses in hagiography, didn't choose Joan of Arc, the image of the nation in arms, who would not be canonized until 1920, but "little Thérèse," the icon of universal compassion, who spent her brief anonymous life at the Carmel of Lisieux in the flame of supernatural hope alone. It was her, and no one else, whom countless soldiers, who initially believed in Heaven or didn't,[2] requested to go with them throughout four years of fighting that felt like hell on earth.

Reaching French, Belgian, English, even German men, from private to officer, from cook to chaplain, from agnostic to practicing Christian, the adolescent who had sung the love of God thus inspired a wave of devotion, not distinguishable from a new or renewed conversion, to the most simple and the most immediate virtues of humanity within a dehumanized conflict.

[1] *Poilu* (literally "hairy man"): nickname of the French private in the trenches.

[2] *Celui qui croyait au ciel/Celui qui n'y croyait pas*, "He who believed in Heaven/He who didn't": this is the first line of a poem by French poet Louis Aragon (*La Rose et le Réséda*), written in the context of the French Resistance during World War II and famously quoted by French writer and minister of culture André Malraux in the funeral oration of Jean Moulin, a member of the Resistance.

In the face of the "Grim Reaper," of the ghastly sight of an endless massacre, and of the prevalent feeling of an imminent apocalypse, many of them wanted to testify to this unheard-of meeting with salvation, all the more unexpected as they seemed doomed to death, a salvation personified by Saint Thérèse. To express their gratitude to her, unable as they were to pay her a visit on pilgrimage, they wrote to her.

More than 2,000 thematic files are kept at the Carmel of Lisieux, containing the handwritten letters received throughout the Great War—up to around a hundred a day —but also decorations, trophies, medallions, bullets, helmets, and shells transformed into ex-votos. All these items constitute an exceptional repository of the popular mindset, piety, and art, as well as a singular memorial of France and of the French of that era, bringing back to life a bygone world. But it also conveys a message for these days.

By displaying seventy-five of these missives, all typical of a religious impetus ignored by historians so far, this volume does not only pursue a devotional aim. For beyond her miraculous interventions, it is Thérèse's mystical presence on the battlefields that makes it invaluable, referring us to this transcendental dimension inherent to the history of men, which, she shows, is ineluctable. The most humble of saints gives hope again to these humiliated men for whom despair feels like damnation. At a time when one of the main tragedies of the contemporary world, overwhelmed by conflicts and technology, is lack of confidence, these letters by *Poilus*, wrested from the lower depths, prove that there is a supreme power of the mind, "stronger than steel."

THE
LETTERS

I don't know you, but…

On September 7, at the battle of the Marne,[1] the 2nd Battalion of the —th Infantry Regiment was given the order to support the advance of two other battalions nearby, and to attack the village of —, located halfway between Montceaux-lès-Provins and Esternay.[2] At that moment, the battalion was gathered behind a small birch wood; on the other side of the wood, in order to reach the village, we had to cross an open ground made of two large fields, a stalk field and an alfalfa one. It was no easy business, since these fields were being swept with enemy machine-gun fire and shells; a patrol of five men and an officer had just been mowed down there, with none of them getting back on his feet. The 1st Section of the 8th Company, of which I was part, followed by the other sections, came out of the wood first and deployed as skirmishers advancing in bounds, but the ground had been carefully scouted out by the enemy, which was spraying us copiously with its shells. The rumbling of the shells, the noise they made when they burst, mingled with the whistling of the bullets and the rat-a-tat of the machine guns was such that we literally had to yell to make ourselves heard. We had crossed only 60 meters, and a full third of our troop was already out

---

[1] The first Battle of the Marne took place in September 1914, in the eponymous French "department." It blocked the German advance into France, leading to a war of position on the Western front, a stalemate that was to last until early 1918.

[2] Two cities of the Marne department.

of action. The lieutenant had fallen stone-dead at the first rush, the warrant officer and the sergeant major at the second one. Unable to move forward though backed by other companies, we were holding our ground, waiting for our artillery to arrive; blocked, lying flat on the ground, becoming one with the ground, as it were, we responded as best we could to the shots of the enemy safely sheltered in front of the village and in its first houses.

It was certainly not more than fifteen minutes before we heard over our heads the response our 75[3] were sending to the enemy batteries. The man on my right side had just been killed instantly by a bullet shot right into his head, the man on my left had a leg broken by shrapnel and also a piece of shrapnel in his shoulder. Well, in such circumstances minutes feel like hours, and one's mind works quickly. Never doubting it would soon be my turn, I silently renewed my act of contrition; this is when I remembered the little Sister Thérèse, of whom my mother had given me a relic that I carried with me. I began to invoke her, saying: "Little Sister Thérèse, I don't know you, but Mother prays to you and likes you; if you get me out of this bind, I'll go on a pilgrimage to Lisieux and will do all that I can to spread your name within my circle of friends and relatives." I then resumed shooting, waiting for the shot that would hit me, and... it never came. A few moments later, backed by a new battery pulling down the houses where the Germans had taken refuge, we launched

[3] The 75 mm shells, specific to the French artillery. Shells were commonly referred to by their caliber.

an attack on the village and took it, while the enemy was hastily leaving the place.

Since that day, I have experienced tough affairs[4] many times; none of them, however, ever compared with what happened on September 7, because we had to fight on open ground. I most definitely owe my life to the protection of the little Sister, to whom I have kept praying ever since in all difficult times. No need to say that, having obtained a leave following an illness, I went to Lisieux to thank the little Sister and request her assistance for the future, and sent relics to all my comrades at the front. They were received with gratitude.

CdOUNT OF BÉRENGER

---

[4] "An affair," in WWI lingo, was a battle, or any action involving fighting.

Bless my soul! Was not some little novena made here?

Wounded on October 1, 1914, by a piece of shrapnel in my left leg, I was evacuated and hospitalized at Saint-Hilaire-du-Harcouët (Manche),[1] where I arrived on October 4.

At first sight, the doctor thought it was a superficial, not too serious cut; nonetheless, I was examined by means of X-rays, which showed, at the time, no trace of a foreign body.

After a fortnight stay at the hospital, however, since the cut wouldn't heal and ached more and more, I complained to the doctor who, this time, examined me by means of a probe, an intervention that led him to think there was a projectile in my leg, or bone decay. On October 22, I underwent a radioscopic examination that revealed the presence of a "foreign body" in the tibiotarsal articulation. A surgery to extract the projectile was therefore decided upon, and was scheduled for Sunday, October 25, 1914.

On the morning of the appointed day, the extraction of the projectile—which had lodged itself in the fibula—was carried out, as well as the curettage of the bone. That evening, and on the following days, I suffered horribly, and, distressingly enough, in spite of the most devoted care, my poor foot was becoming a hideous sight, assuming various tints of black, yellow, blue, etc., so that the doctors—there were three of them—having decided upon an amputation and considering it essential, not to say unavoidable, very carefully hinted to me that we would

---

[1] French department of La Manche in Normandy.

probably have to come to it. I will not mention my moments of despair, and the thousands of kindnesses of the good sisters, who lavished attention on me in this critical time, and whom I shall never forget!

In spite of the decision they had made, the doctors hesitated when it was observed I was consumed by fever, while I was in a state of extreme weakness; this is when my good sisters had a wonderful idea and thought of making a novena to Sister Thérèse of the Child Jesus, after placing a relic of Lisieux on the condemned foot.

As soon as the following day, a perceptible improvement was noticed; as for me, I was feeling much better; the doctor, the head physician, having come to observe my condition, was so surprised to see such improvement that he commented before the sisters: "Bless my soul! Was not some little novena made here?" To which the Reverend Mother answered back: "Do you believe in novenas, Doctor?" "Yes," he replied, "when the patient himself has faith in them!" And the Reverend Mother replied: "This may well be the case!" My faith was indeed unlimited. It was a good thing, because today I am radically—one might even say miraculously—cured by the little sister Thérèse of the Child Jesus.

E. Saint-Joanis,
soldier, 92nd Infantry Regiment,
26th Company, in Clermont-Ferrand
(Puy-de-Dôme)[2]

---

[2] Puy-de-Dôme, a department located in the French volcanic mountain Massif Central.

I saw a cloud open up

Reverend Mother,

As I came and told you in Lisieux, on October 21, I am a
protégé of the little Thérèse of the Child Jesus and have
great confidence in her. I visited her grave in May 1914,
and came back deeply impressed. Nonetheless, when war
was declared, I resisted my wife's entreaties and left without going to confession. It was human respect that held
me back in the fulfilment of my Christian duties. I had
gone astray from the Church since my first communion. I
accepted, however, a relic and an image of the little sister,
and every time I found myself in danger during battles, I
instinctively called upon her for help and noticed that
each time she protected me and my comrades, for I never
saw any of them killed or wounded right next to me.

Roughly in mid-September, we were lying flat in the
trenches of the Gotha, near Reims.[1]

It was a difficult time, for the two artilleries kept thun-
dering.

I was thinking mournfully of my little family and said
to Sister Thérèse: "My sister Thérèse, give me back, I
beseech you, to my wife and children, and I promise to
visit your grave as soon as I am back home."

---

[1] French town of the Marne department. The trenches of the Gotha
led to Verdun.

No sooner had I said this prayer than *I saw a cloud open up and the face of the saint stand out against the blue sky.* I thought I was the victim of some hallucination. I rubbed my eyes several times, staring again at the vision, but I could have absolutely no doubt, since her face was more and more distinct and resplendent. I could contemplate her this way for one or two minutes. *I particularly noticed her most beautiful eyes, lifted heavenward as if to pray.* Since that time, I have always been courageous, I haven't felt lonely anymore. I have also had the strongest hope of seeing my loved ones again and have kept alive an unwavering resolution to return to the God of my childhood.

Indeed, a short time afterward, when I was evacuated due to sickness, and when, at the hospital where I was being treated, it was asked who wanted to receive communion, I wasn't afraid of showing my desire, and I promised straight off that I would always fulfill my Easter duties.

Use this letter as you see fit, Reverend Mother, I am no more ashamed; on the contrary, I am proud to bear witness to the goodness of God and of Sister Thérèse toward a poor sinner.

AUGUSTE COUSINARD
*reservist, 5th infantry
Regiment from Falaise*[2]

[2] A town in Normandy, not far from Lisieux.

Battery Sister Thérèse

Letter passed on to the Carmel of Lisieux by the grandmother and the mother of its writer, on December 28, 1914.

As you know, I have carried with me Sister Thérèse's little relic since the beginning of the war, and here is what happened to me.

On the last day we fought in the Marne, in September, we were facing the enemy with only eight cannons, while the Germans had twenty-five of them. At this critical time we were lacking ammunition, and when we ceased firing, in our haste to move other carriages forward in our place, I fell down in such an unfortunate way that my cannon passed over both my legs; they should have been entirely crushed, for our 75 weighed 4000 pounds! At this point my dear brothers in arms hurried to me to transport me. How astonished they were, when they saw me get up unscathed! They all cried: "Miracle! Miracle!" To which I immediately replied, with such gratefulness in my heart: "I owe it to my little Thérèse." And right away, pulling a white pencil out of my pocket, I wrote in big letters on my cannon:

> *Battery Sister Thérèse*
> *of the Child Jesus*

Since that day, when it rains and the name fades, I redo it as soon as I can. I have boundless confidence in the protection of this saint.

PAUL DUGAST,
gun pointer,[1] *51st Artillery Regiment*

---

[1] Literally *maître pointeur*, a distinction with no English equivalent awarded to particularly gifted and experienced artillery pointers.

The voice of Sister Thérèse

At Landremont, I occupied a room where I found, placed above the mantelpiece, the portrait of Sister Thérèse of the Child Jesus, a saint I already knew and prayed to with confidence and for whose beatification I pray to God every day. I got into the habit of praying my rosary before this image. Well, on the evening of September 16, my prayer was suddenly interrupted in the following way. I very distinctly heard a voice saying to me, at intervals: "You will be wounded before the end of the month… you will be badly wounded… but all the less so because, from this day forward, you will accept this sacrifice generously for God."

The voice, which imposed itself on my mind during more than a quarter of an hour was, I felt, Sister Thérèse's.

Try as I might to resume my vocal prayer, I still perceived the same warning, so that I said aloud: "My God, I accept in advance all it will please you to send me." That was what Sister Thérèse wanted, for I could finish my rosary right away; but when I went to bed, the memory of what had occurred kept coming to my mind, and on the following morning I wrote it down in my notebook.

We experienced heavy fighting on October 7 and 17. Eventually, on the evening of the twentieth, just when I was getting ready to relieve a company in the first-line trenches, the regiment was given the order to get ready for an attack that should take place on the following day, in the wood of Mort-Mare,[1] before dawn. My reserve company was to be sacrificed, if need be, to take ground in that wood. I was issued an order to that effect. When I received the last instructions before battle, I said to the commandant: "We are heading for death." And such was my conviction, not only for my own troop, but also for the whole regiment.

On October 21, at around 3 a.m., while we were advancing toward the muster point, I was reflecting on the events that were to take place in a few moments, and on what could happen to me. So I said this prayer again: "O Lord, do with me as you will." Three hours later, I received four bullets and was transported to the rear.

Besides relatively light wounds, the radius of my right arm was broken and my hand was transpierced; the radial artery, however, was not at all damaged—if it had, it could have resulted in a hemorrhage, possibly a lethal one. Moreover, on the spot where the bullet got out, in spite of the ravages it produced, no tendon was cut, so that I will keep the use of all my fingers.

How much I have to thank God and Sister Thérèse for so obviously protecting me! As soon as I arrived in the hospital of Toul,[2] I promised to write all about it to the Carmel of Lisieux.

Admittedly, I expected to be wounded in the end of

[1] The wood of Mort-Mare is located in the vicinity of Verdun. It was the scene of several military operations, especially in April 1915 during the Battle of Verdun. The present letter, however, refers to the very beginning of trench warfare, in the fall of 1914.

[2] A French town, situated in the portion of Lorraine territory left to France in 1870.

September, since the voice had told me: "You will be wounded in the end of the month." But for divinely wise reasons, I am in no doubt about it, God considered it inappropriate to reveal to me in the end of which month I would see the fulfillment of the prophecy. Therefore I will never forget the event I consider a huge grace, and, if it can be useful to the glorification of Sister Thérèse, I gladly accept that it should be published.

CAPTAIN MASTER,
captain, 232nd Infantry Regiment,
Knight of the Legion of Honor [3]

---

[3] Legion of Honor (*Légion d'Honneur*): the highest French order of merit for military and civil merits. There are several degrees of distinction: Knight, Officer, Commander, Grand Officer, Grand Cross.

She was on her knees

In the English Army, February 25, 1915

I, Corporal James Dalton, of the Royal Dublin Fusiliers, went to the front on September 11, 1914. I have a great devotion to the Little Flower of Jesus, Sister Thérèse, and never let a day pass without invoking her.

On an evening of October 1914, about six or half past six, I was in the trenches. At this moment we were not shooting, because the artillery was in action on both sides.

I prayed to the Little Flower, and suddenly *a nun appeared before me*, six or seven feet away from me. *She was very beautiful and was on her knees, her head bent and her hands folded; but her face wore an expression of intense sadness, as if she deeply pitied us.* I recognized at once the saint of Lisieux. This happened at Hiplines, near Armentières.[1]

A few weeks later, I saw her again twice, in the same attitude, as if praying for us, and I feel her effective protection surrounding me every day.

JAMES DALTON, *lance corporal*
FR. FARRINGTON, *priest*

---

[1] Armentières, in northern France, was the scene of an important battle in 1914.

The relic sewn inside their greatcoat

At the front, February 25, 1915

Reverend Mother,

I received from His Lordship the Count of Montozon-Brachet relics of Sister Thérèse of the Child Jesus, and I can't resist telling you how much luck they bring us.

I am but a mere corporal, promoted under enemy fire, but I wish I were more than that, so that my rank would allow me to spread on a broader scale the propaganda I am creating within my own group.

All my men have sewn inside their greatcoat the relic that performs so many miracles, and I am certain, Reverend Mother, that you will appreciate the little story I am going to tell you.

Fifteen meters away from the German trenches, we have a post made of two squads, which relieve each other on alternate days.

For four days, in all the squads occupying this post, there were men killed, and many wounded. When our turn came, I started very peacefully, putting all my trust in God, and during this two days of danger, my men and I prayed fervently, saying, among others, the prayer of the little Sister Thérèse. Well, neither a bomb nor a grenade fell on us, and no sooner did we leave the post than the horrible hail of bullets started again, battering those who were replacing us. Good Christians that we are, we all feel that some protection from above envelops us.

At night, at the bivouac, we often gather to read a portion of the *Life* of Sister Thérèse, and this is the most beautiful moment of our day, in this ghastly upheaval. No fear of any of us interrupting the reader, and the noise of the cannon hardly disturbs us. Several of my comrades are harassing me to have a medallion of our saint; Reverend Mother, you'll find their names hereby attached, which they would gladly sign with both hands, to express their gratitude to you. I therefore rely on your kindness to satisfy them.

Yours faithfully,

JEAN-CHARLES ATGER,
corporal, 111th Infantry Regiment,
3rd Company

Sudden healing

From the Yser front,[1] March 3, 1915

Reverend Mother,

It is a protégé of your little saint who is writing to you; I may have been too slow to pay my debt of gratitude, but at last I can assure you that the following fact, which I noted down in my logbook at the time it happened, is true.

It was on September 16, 1914. The Battle of the Marne was over; the Battle of the Aisne[2] was beginning. Tired by an exhausting retreat and hard fighting, we had spent the night at Cauroy-lès-Hermonville, not far from the famous plateau of Craonne.[3] But, as soon as day broke, we had to prepare for departure.

I was extremely tired and, to crown it all, my right foot was all skinned and even inflamed, so much so that I could not bear the shoe. I therefore found myself incapable of marching on.

This is when the little Sister Thérèse came to my mind, and taking her image, I placed it on the cut, with the utmost confidence. I then put my shoe back on and went marching again.

[1] The front near the river Yser, in Belgium, was the scene of one of the first battles in Flanders, in 1914.

[2] The first Battle of the Aisne, in northern France, took place in September 1914, in the wake of the Battle of the Marne.

[3] After the first Battle of the Aisne, the village of Craonne, located on the front line, was occupied by the Germans.

Extraordinarily, after a few moments, I felt my foot all wet, and not the slightest pain! In about five or six minutes, and right on the march, my cut had healed! I verified the fact as soon as I could: the limb was perfectly healthy and bore no mark of harm.

Most certainly, the fatigues of this painful day could not have brought about this sudden healing; from a human point of view, on the contrary they should necessarily have delayed it. But the hand of the little saint had touched me!

FERNAND DUCOM,
corporal, 2nd Engineering Regiment,
Company 1912

Severed neck

Béthune,[1] March 21, 1915

To the Reverend Mother Superior of the Carmel of Lisieux

Reverend Mother,

I was delighted to receive a few weeks ago the little pamphlet containing excerpts from letters you received, which show the great power of our little sister Thérèse of the Child Jesus.

I would fail in the great duty of gratefulness if I too didn't expound to you how this little saint, who will someday be the patron of our Normandy,[2] preserved my life so that I could return to my loved ones.

When I was called by mobilization to defend our dear homeland, I knew nothing about Sister Thérèse. Shortly after I departed, a cousin of mine, a very pious soul, more advanced than I am, sent me the prayer and the image of the little saint. Every day in the trench, I invoked Sister Thérèse and said the prayer for her beatification, my eyes set toward her heavenly dwelling. I carried her image on my heart and had unlimited trust in her; I assure you I feared nothing, I felt invulnerable.

---

[1] Béthune, in northern France, was half destroyed by bombardments during the war, but was never occupied by the Germans.

[2] Lisieux is located in Normandy. Saint Thérèse of the Child Jesus actually was declared secondary patron of France in 1944.

It was the little sister's will that I received my glorious wound while we were fighting in Artois.[3]

Under a spray of bullets, I picked up wounded men and carried them on my back; I did it without fear, for I had my good guardian with me. I had just left a wounded man in the hands of the stretcher-bearers when a shell cut my neck very deeply, over a length of 14 or 15 centimeters, and floored me.

I felt my blood flowing out abundantly, my eyes were blacking out, my ears were ringing, my arm and my shoulder as though torn off and inert, I thought my final hour had come. At this moment, my thoughts rose toward Heaven, toward the Servant of God, whom I accused of ingratitude; I here transcribe the exact expression of my thoughts: "How is that, little Sister Thérèse of the Child Jesus, you abandon me, who have invoked you every single day since I have known you!"

My eyes immediately could see the light of day again, and I had the strength to get up and, very bloody, my arm twitching (for all the muscles joining the shoulder to the neck were cut), to bid farewell to my men and to exhort them as they were about to attack.

With an effort, I managed to return to the trench, where a stretcher-bearer received me into his arms; he hastily bandaged my wound and dragged me to the dressing sta-

---

[3] Artois is the name of a traditional French province, corresponding to the modern department of Pas-de-Calais, in the North of the country. The Battle of Artois took place May–June 1915. Since the letter dates back to March 1915, the soldier is referring to less important fighting in the area.

tion; we stopped on our way under a small bridge, we had barely left our shelter when a shell knocked it down.

The various doctors who treated me have always wondered by what miracle my head was still on my shoulders and how the carotid artery had not been cut; I was considered a phenomenon.

I was tended to in Deauville[4] by the very devoted, very religious, very gentle Sister Mechtilde, of the Franciscan Order; she could tell you what a horrible wound she so well treated and cured.

Here is, Reverend Mother, what I wanted to tell you out of gratitude.

I allow you to use my letter and my name, and I will consider my debt to be reduced in some measure if I have been able to help you have the little Servant of God known and honored.

I remain, Reverend Mother, your most sincere and respectful servant.

V. DEGRÉMONT,
sublieutenant, 329th Infantry Regiment of Le Havre,[5]
Knight of the Legion of Honor, nominated twice

---

[4] A town in Normandy.
[5] A town in northwest France.

I was busy tasting my beans

May 3, 1915

My dear little sister,

I promised you yesterday I would tell you exactly how this bullet made its way to me. Well, it's very simple. We were in the wood of A., in the first-line trenches.[1] Since I cook for my officers and since the hut they spend the night in is by no means large or luxurious, I had the idea of piercing a bucket and doing my cooking outside, with charcoal of course, since there must be no smoke 200 meters away from the Boches.[2] So I was busy tasting my beans, at 10 a.m. on April 15, crouching near my pots, when a bullet arrived, went through two boxes in front of my pot, passed above my forefinger, went through the bucket I use as a furnace, sending ash into my eyes and passed 4 or 5 centimeters away from my thigh, where the packet with the image of Sister Thérèse was. I can tell you I have prayed to her every day; but since that event I assure you I have not only prayed to her, but have kissed her image every single day, for I firmly believe I was protected. And please thank the good sisters for me, until I do my duty in regard to this event [i.e., make a pilgrimage or an offering].

Pray for me always.

HENRI BRETON

[1] There were several sorts of trenches. First-line trenches, or main fire trenches were those in close contact with the enemy on the front line, as opposed to communication trenches, and support lines, where the dugouts were situated.

[2] The Boches: offensive trench lingo nickname for the Germans.

The relic replaces the doctor

Volunteer hospital of Vinça[1]
June 9, 1915

I, the undersigned Constant Beaudeau, declare I received shrapnel in my right thigh, on March 5, 1915. The doctors were worried and hesitated to extract it, saying they could not do it without touching the sciatic nerve. So a nurse, Miss Rose Vernis, had the fortunate idea of placing on my dressing a relic of Sister Thérèse of the Child Jesus, and on the following day the piece of shrapnel had gone out of the wound all by itself. Therefore, out of gratitude I never forget to decorate with flowers the image of Sister Thérèse, in whom I will always have faith.

CONSTANT BEAUDEAU
ROSE VERNIS, *nurse*
M. BÈS-PINET, *nurse*

[1] Vinça: a town in Southern France, near the Spanish border. A "voluntary hospital" (*hôpital bénévole*) was set up on private initiative.

Touched by joy

Dear Mother Prioress,

It is with great joy that I send you this letter, to thank you deeply, with all my heart, for the little samples I received from your kindness on the twenty-fourth of this month. Dear Mother, I was touched by joy when these little pictures caught my eye, I felt an impression that renewed my morale; but I was not the only one. One of my men who was near me was struck in the same way, and found the little picture so nice that he asked me at once if I had any others, and for how much I would sell them. Seeing him so touched, and so happy to get acquainted with Little Sister Thérèse, I gave him a cardboard picture and a medallion. He was so happy that he couldn't help glancing at the medallion all the time. Very soon, a man of my squad, who was sitting not far from us, got wind of this little delivery, approached me and asked me if I had any of these medallions left; I gave him the last one at once. So the three medallions are in my squad, entrusted to reliable hands, and they have unrestricted confidence in this little saint. Several of my comrades came from time to time and asked if I had medallions. When I told them I didn't, their smiling faces grew sad; but since they asked me to send some to them right away, it makes me happy myself to make others happy and to meet their newfound confidence in this little Sister Thérèse.

Dear Mother, I send you, attached to this letter, a five francs banknote, which I hope will reach you, since I can't have a money order for it. I offer two francs to the little Sister Thérèse of the Child Jesus, which you can use as you please, and I beg you to kindly join me in my thanksgiving for her good deeds toward me so far. I think these little medallions are worth 0.20 francs each, I will therefore ask you to kindly send me seven medallions at once, so that I can satisfy several of my eager friends. And I beg you to excuse me for the trouble I am giving you, dear Mother. I have a wife and two little daughters, a seven year old and a six year old, who are presently at Saint-Germain-de-Mont-gommery,[1] I beg you to kindly send three medallions to my very dear beloved ones, which leads us to a total of ten medallions, 0.20 francs each.

Medallions: 2 francs
2 francs of offering: 2 francs
There remains therefore 1 franc for the postage: 1 franc
Total: 5 francs

Here is the address of my wife: Mrs. Bellois Adrienne at Saint-Germain-de-Montgommery near Vimoutiers (Calvados, Orne). I couldn't easily send little medallions to my wife; this is why I beg you to send them to her. I thank you in advance with all my heart, together with my comrades.

Dear Mother, please accept my warm greetings.

Your devoted champion,

HENRI BELLOIS,
corporal, 304th Regiment,
21st Company, postal sector no. 149

---

[1] A French town in Normandy, not far from Lisieux.

Minenwerfer[1]

I had 80 men out of action, out of the 157 I had taken with me, and brought back only one officer out of four, the three other ones having been killed.

Long live Little Sister Thérèse, my Johanette,[2] and long live the French blood that could prove to the Germans nothing would give them victory.

Now that I am having some respite, I can give you a few details about the events of the morning of June 30th, a morning that will forever be engraved in my memory, the details of which are still very clear in my mind.

As for the men I brought back, their morale is wonderful and better than ever.

Here's the scene: I had been in the first-line trenches of —, about 500 meters to the west of B., since June 27 at 1 a.m. On the twenty-eighth, the Germans began firing on us with 210 guns (which are large-caliber pieces) and on the twenty-ninth sent huge *Minenwerfer* on the two companies that surrounded me on the right and on the left.

I even told my officers: "The Germans have been attacking unsuccessfully for about one month on the right and on the left. If I were them, I would attack at the center; well, we are the center; so beware!"

The night of the twenty-ninth to the thirtieth was rather calm. I had just stretched out at my command post, when

[1] *Minenwerfer*: German for "mine launcher."
[2] First name of his female addressee.

around 2, I was awakened by the fall of a big *Minenwerfer*, then complete silence... I took the opportunity to have a stroll in my trench; everything was silent, the men on duty watchful at their posts, the other ones having a rest. I joined my post at around half past three; at four, that is at dawn, the massed volley began suddenly:[3] I first received a salvo of 20 or 30 shells, several of which fell right next to my post; believing it extended all along the parapet of my trench, I dashed in to the telephone post, which was in an outside hut a few meters away, intending to inform the sector commander, but... though the bombardment started only five minutes before, all communications were interrupted. From that moment on, the German artillery firing reached *astounding* intensity; my telephonic post was smashed to pieces, then collapsed; I was certainly receiving more than 120 to 150 shells a minute, as much on my trench as on my commanding post. I sent a liaison officer[4] to the rear in order to explain what was going on, but I knew he was doomed to death!

After half an hour, the entrance of my post had received so many shells that it was almost obstructed. My orderly continually scratched with his hands to make the earth go down inside the post, so that I always have a small hole to get out through, in the manner of a snake; I kept relighting a candle that was continually put out by explosions and the

[3] Massive artillery barrages usually took place before infantry attacks, preferably at night so as to achieve an element of surprise.

[4] Liaison officers, in charge of delivering messages to other sectors of the front, played a crucial role, since telephone lines were often damaged or unavailable, and radio transmission was still in its infancy.

displacement of air produced by shells of all calibers that were ceaselessly falling down before what remained of my exit hole.

At half past five, the artillery abruptly stopped firing. I immediately crawled out of my post and ran to the trench to inspect the damages. Gunfire crackled, the Germans were attacking; I had several Boches in my trench, and I saw several wounded being transported to my post. The Germans quickly noticed that their artillery had not smashed us all; our firing was harming them, so that they went to the ground, and the bombardment continued, as intensely as the first one. My trench was bombarded from one end to the other by a battery of 105, among many others that caused huge damages and brought about heavy casualties; more than twenty shells fell down and burst less than 4 meters away from me.

D., one of my lieutenants, who is by my side, then told me: "Captain, you can't stay here, you're going to be killed; your duty, anyway, is to go back to your commanding post." After an intense salvo, I returned to my post, which was crowded with wounded men, and crawled my way inside it.

Shortly afterwards, a 210 shell fell on my post and partly smashed it—though it was still livable. I had been invoking Sister Thérèse for a long time. I was amazed at my own calm. But it was probably because I realized completely that I couldn't get out of it without a miracle.

At seven o'clock, there was a new abrupt stop of the artillery; gunfire started again, the machine guns crackled. The Germans probably noticed very quickly that not all of us were out of action, so that five minutes afterward shell-fire started again with more intensity, and the shells kept pouring down for one more hour.

Then the German artillery stopped firing. The Germans attempted their third attack, which was now easy for them; there remained nothing of my trench, which was completely shattered, a frightful chaos. They couldn't penetrate frontally, though, and outflanked me on the right and on the left. We fought by means of grenades and bombs. At last, someone shouted to me: "You are being outflanked! Withdraw, for God's sake!"

I therefore withdrew, but my poor remaining men moved forward as best they could, since the communication trenches were obstructed by lacerated fallen trees, by heaps of earth, etc. We crossed 200 or 300 meters this way, under machine-gun fire; we then arrived under the frightful barrage the German artillery was performing on our reserves.

I persisted in walking down the communication trench, for enormous 150 and 210 shells kept falling nearby, mowing everything down and covering me with earth when they burst very close to me. The communication trench offered cover. X. and Z. were going ahead of me. The former, at a difficult spot where the trench was almost filled and covered with a tree, went over the top, and afterwards I saw no more of him. Poor Z. then lost patience, and doing a pull-up, jumped out of the trench; I attempted to do the same, but failed. At this moment a shell skimmed past me and brought poor Z. down.

I waited... and when the trench disgorged, I saw at some distance my poor disemboweled lieutenant lying down.

At last I arrived in a ravine that provided some respite;

shells were still pouring down there, but what is a 210 falling 50 meters away, when you have seen so many brush past you?

But the respite didn't last long, for I had hardly joined a few men when a gas shell fell 20 meters away from us.

At last, somewhat suffocated, with tears in my eyes, I managed to gather the remains of my poor squadron in the hollow of the ravine. There were only 52 of my poor dragoons left. It was by this time nine in the morning.

In the afternoon, I assigned them to supply with ammunition counterattacking troops that were successfully repelling the enemy's dreadful efforts everywhere, and at midnight I received the order to join the flanking maneuver, which was bound to happen anyway. I also was able to collect a few wounded…

This affair caused the following casualties: it cost me eight men and three officers, killed, wounded or missing. For there certainly were some of my badly wounded men who couldn't be evacuated to the rear and remained in the trenches—or were buried under the collapsed parapets.[5]

I can assure you that when a man has gone through such a trial and has escaped unharmed, he can no longer doubt divine Providence. For I am certain that more than a hundred shells passed or burst less than 5 meters away from me. It is therefore absolutely miraculous that no shrapnel even grazed me.

At some point, for instance, in the ravine, feeling that a shell was coming down on me, I could huddle against a

[5] Men buried alive in collapsed trenches were, sadly, one of the horrors of the Great War.

big tree. Well, the shell fell one meter away from the tree, and all the shrapnel brushed by me.

Another 210 shell, while I was in a communication trench, uprooted a proud oak less than 10 meters away from me; I will always have engraved in my memory the sight of this beautiful oak collapsing, becoming the center of an enormous spray of shards, pebbles, scrap iron, etc. It was otherworldly.

I still recommend silence concerning the names of my poor dear killed officers. We have to wait till their families are informed.[6]

LAURENCIN

[6] It was indeed against military regulation to directly inform the family of a fallen soldier before an official death announcement was made by the army.

The Little Flower

I am very pleased to tell you about two extraordinary protections carried out by the Little Flower. The first one happened on February 6, 1915, at G. We had been commanded to attack a German position. Everything was prepared, and we were waiting for our artillery to stop bombarding before it was our turn to charge. Our time eventually arrived; my men were a little pale. Before we departed, I beseeched the Little Flower to give me much courage and to bring me back to my beloved mother. I pulled my image out of my pocket and, holding it in my hand, jumped over the parapet of the trench onto the prairie. Thousands of projectiles soon passed near me at frightening speed. Bullets were sinking into the earth at my feet. An officer on my right and another soldier on my left were killed; as for me, I was able to go forward unwounded to our new position.

The Little Flower protected me again in a wonderful way. It was on May 18, 1915. Our artillery had started a dreadful bombardment. It seemed almost impossible to stay alive while this lasted. As I was fastening my bayonet to the barrel of my rifle, I very distinctly heard (in spite of the roar of the shells bursting all around us) a voice, the sweetest voice I ever heard in my life, which was whispering in my ears: "Take my relic." As in a dream, I put my hand in my pocket and took the little relic. With this weapon, I felt another man and, upon receiving the order

40

to attack, I rushed forward ardently. After reaching our goal, we spent the night safely sheltered at X. I noticed that half of the soldiers of my company were killed or wounded. While we were sleeping, a shell burst and killed several men by my side. All of a sudden I felt hit myself in my leg and in my chest. What was I to do? It seemed impossible to go back to the trenches without being killed. I faithfully prayed to Sister Thérèse, and again heard the same voice telling me: "Go back, go back." So I obeyed, and, still holding the relic in my hand, I crawled back to the trench, while the shells were bursting so close to me than I sometimes was almost suffocated by the smoke. But they had no effect upon me.

Thanks be to the Little Flower.

J. G. MULQUEEN,
sergeant,
1st Battalion Irish Guards

Hell

Dear Cousin,

Before I embark upon a long relation of all that just happened to me, will you allow me to raise a thought of thanksgiving toward our little saint?

O good little sister Saint Thérèse of the Child Jesus, who recently had mercy on my two dear little daughters by so overtly granting that my life should be spared, I thank you with all my heart and renew the vow I took on the dreadful battlefield to visit your grave as soon as I can, and to give testimony of your intervention whenever I will be asked to! O you, who are so close to God, tell him how great my gratitude is, and about me, tell him I will do everything possible so that my children keep loving him, blessing him and being grateful to him for what he just did for us, through your intercession!

Now, my dear cousin, here is what just happened to me:

I have just escaped from death in such an extraordinary way that it would be absurd not to acknowledge the hand of God, prayed to by his holy Servant. On October 26, at six in the morning, we received the order to launch an attack on the German trench. There was a thick fog; we didn't really know where this trench was. So, I got out with all the men of my section, and at the moment the order was issued, while I was going over the top,[1] after giv-

---

[1] "To go over the top," in trench lingo, was to go over the trench's parapet and launch an attack.

ing my own orders to my men I thought about God in my inmost self, and here is what I told him, or words to that effect: "My God, I love you, forgive me my trespasses, and your will be done," and just after that: "Little Sister Saint Thérèse, have mercy on my children, and if such be the will of God, grant that I be given back to them, by saving my life. I will go to Lisieux to visit your grave and I will give testimony at the Carmel of the favor you obtained for me."

This is more or less what I was thinking, and you will see how things went on.

So, we went into the attack with our saber in one hand, our revolver in the other. We crossed 100 meters in the fog and then, ah! my poor cousin, if only you could have seen that! The Germans we thought we were attacking frontally were actually on our right. This is when a spray of bullets fell less than 60 meters away from us; rifles, machine guns to the max, and in our flank position we couldn't respond. There was only one thing left to do: to change front and hurl ourselves at them. My men were dropping like flies. Anyway, in the surrounding noise, amidst the cries of pain of the dying and wounded men, I managed in no time at all to gather the remaining troops and I rushed into the German trench. We were not running—we couldn't anymore, we were so out of breath; oh well, we had to be content with walking; and at the moment we were about to catch them, a last burst of gunfire mowed down what remained of my men, fewer than three or four of them; too bad, but we kept walking forward, and that was when I received an astounding blow of a bludgeon to my head, almost at point-blank range. I tottered a few moments and was thrown with dreadful violence into a shell hole that fortunately enough happened to be there. I was losing floods of blood. Two other wounded men joined me in this hole; one of them had his leg blown away by an explosive bullet, the other one was literally riddled with machine-gun bullets. A third wounded man was trying to reach this hole, but he was immediately finished off before he succeeded; a fourth wounded man, seeing the fate of his comrades, laid down on his stomach and played dead for a while. Unfortunately, we were too close to the German trench, barely 4 or 5 meters. The poor devil moved. The Boches saw him and that was when a scene of unheard-of savagery occurred. A machine gun was aimed at him and about every other minute, the scoundrels sent a bullet into his head! To think I was there powerless, what torment! What's more, one of the wounded in my hole entered his death throes; it was the one who had been riddled with bullets. At last he died, from loss of blood. I don't know why, but at this point I had not lost consciousness; my blood, however, was still flowing out and I was feeling weak. I remembered that I had mint alcohol; I quickly swallowed a few drops of it and gave a good draft to the other wounded man by my side, who was also losing floods of blood. The sight of all this blood reminded me of my own condition, for I clearly felt I was losing my strength. I quickly grasped my first-aid pouch and almost succeeded in stopping the hemorrhage in my head. My poor dear cousin, what a nightmare! Twelve hours I spent with dead and dying men in at least 20 to 25 centimeters of blood, under a torrid sun with three corpses, one of which was lying over me, and I had no strength left to move it aside. I prayed to God again and felt I was going to fall asleep. I quickly reacted, for it seemed to me it would mean death. The other wounded man was also passing away from loss of blood. I heard him calling to his wife and children, and he often talked to me. Several times he asked me to finish him off—it's horrible! At last he whispered: "O my God, who are so good!" I had a flash of clarity and said to him at once: "Are you a believer?" "Yes," he said. I then encouraged him to pray to God. I think that was what he did, for I could see his poor lips moving. He eventually died at five. Anyway, at last came the night; I said a prayer again and got out of my hole. The Germans spotted me almost immediately and fired at me from all sides, but it was night-time, and crawling on my hands, my stomach, and my knees, at last I successfully reached the French lines. Safe!

Blessed be thou, O Lord!

Now, what exactly had happened to me? It's very simple: a bullet had hit me right in the head, on the right side above my ear in my helmet (for we wear helmets now[2]), through which it had gone. Logically, the bullet should have gone right through my head and come out again around the left ear.

Well it didn't! It went off course, round the helmet, tearing the lining and plowing into my head till the bone without damaging it too much, to come out again behind my head on the left, at the bottom of the helmet. I have kept

[2] The French infantry was the first army corps to wear helmets. The steel "Adrian helmet" was issued in 1915, as a response to the high rate of lethal head wounds caused by shrapnel, a sad feature of modern warfare.

my helmet; I will show it to you. Well, my dear cousin, where many see mere chance, I see something else! I simply see the hand of God, appealed to by our little saint. So be sure that as soon as I can, I will keep my promise, and this could perhaps happen soon.

Yours affectionately, my dear cousin, I'm looking forward to hearing from you.

V. Dardet,
warrant officer,
247th Infantry Regiment,
23rd Company

Embedded in the image

In the Army,[1] October 4, 1915

Reverend Mother,

Since I have been at the front, I have always carried with me the image of Sister Thérèse of the Child Jesus with great confidence, and, having been quite often very exposed, I sincerely believe that this devotion protected me, for I came out of all dangers unscathed.

Once, a bullet grazed my neck, leaving only a burn mark, a second time a piece of shrapnel went through my clothes, my portfolio, the papers that were in it, and stopped on the image of Sister Thérèse, in which it got embedded.

I hereby send you this image as an exhibit, and I give thanks to God and to my dear protector.

Yours faithfully,

CAMILLE MORANGES,
sergeant,
4th Fusiliers,
machine-gun company

---

[1] To prevent the enemy getting wind of proposed tactical moves, soldiers were often forbidden from disclosing the exact position of their units in private correspondence; they therefore resorted to vague phrases such as "at the front," "in the army," etc.

Little Sister Thérèse, save us!

Dear Mother,

I am still in good health, thanks to Sister Thérèse of the Child Jesus, who is protecting me more and more, as well as those who are with me, when I am having a rough time.

Recently, on October 2, at four in the afternoon, I was in my dugout with my warrant officer and a sergeant of my company, when the Germans began pouring heavy shelling on us. A first, then a second shell fell ahead of us, but a third one hit the door spot-on, shaking the dugout till it collapsed; the suffocating gases contained by the shell entered our shelter, and there we were, the three of us, half buried and asphyxiated. When I heard the projectile coming, I cried: "Little Sister Thérèse, save us!" And indeed we have her to thank for escaping entirely unscathed, with only coughing fits. You see, dear Mother, that I am being well protected. We are now only five officers left out of ten in the battalion, so that I now act as captain, and have been commanding the 3rd Company since September 26.

Our infantry men are wonderful; as for my first bayonet attack,[1] which is one of the longest ones ever launched

---

[1] Infantry units sometimes left their trenches in order to attack and hopefully take a portion of the enemy territory, usually no more than a few hundred yards. These attacks often included hand-to-hand fighting, so that soldiers went "over the top" with their bayonets fixed on their rifles, hence the generic name of "bayonet attacks," whether bayonets were actually used in the course of the attack or not.

since the beginning of the war (5 kilometers), it was entirely successful, and every single day I can't help but admire our soldiers, who are happy as larks to comb the countryside, chasing after the Germans, who scurry away before them as rabbits.

I have lost my medal of Sister Thérèse, would you be so kind as to send me another one?

Goodbye, dear Mother, tender greetings from your affectionate son,

LOUIS DE ROMANET

Fathers and sons just as we are

Dear little Aimée,

I'm really surprised to hear you speak as you do about some Prussians, you who are so kind-hearted. Of course not all of them are *that* good, there are mere scoundrels among them. If you could see the houses where they have been! While I'm used to it myself, it makes me shiver with horror, and my heart bleeds when I think of the poor workers who will recover nothing of what is their only possession. But there are French men who are just as cowardly, for they finish all that is left. Don't say: "Those bad Germans;" of course they are the ones who caused our sufferings, but they are being forced to by leaders who compel them to do it. Now, the leaders of the enemy power—they indeed are cursed by their men and by us.

But these poor family fathers! We took one prisoner the other day who has eight young children. These 17-year-old young men who are sent to the battlefield, these young husbands who leave a beloved wife at home, these ones must not be called "the cursed ones," for they cost many tears to their mothers, who struggled so much to bring them up, and they cost just as dearly as we did to give birth to. Doesn't the good Lord, however, love them just as much as he loves us? He didn't create any of us of an inferior race, and we are all just as dear to his heart. So if at times, seeing all their evil doings, I publicly rebel, right away I hear a voice within me saying to me: "Return good for evil, be better than they are," and I go back to my natural feelings and pity them, thinking of the responsibility they will have to face later on. If I am at war, I want to do it honestly and without resentment. If I fight, it is in order not to let my brothers be slaughtered, to help them, since we are under attack. I do it wholeheartedly and quite simply, trying to step aside as much as I can, without ever evading my responsibilities. My officers, however, must have observed it; this is why they selected me for the exceedingly difficult missions, and appear to have some confidence in me. I'm touched by that, but I don't get vain about it since it is my duty. Don't hate the Boches, pray for them.

LE DENEN

She heard my beseeching cry

Reverend Mother,

As an answer to your request, here is a written account of the graces obtained from Sister Thérèse of the Child Jesus; excuse me if I can't express myself in better French, but it comes from the heart.

I will leave Lisieux regretfully, taking with me the unforgettable memory of her who was my protector, and I am sure she will always guide me on a good path. This day of my pilgrimage seems as beautiful to me as the day of my first holy communion. You'll find enclosed my little offering for Sister Thérèse. How I wish I were rich, to give her more!

A soul thankful for so many favors from Sister Thérèse,

J. LALLEMENT
sergeant,
3rd Foot Artillery Regiment,
4th Battery

Under oath, I affirm I owe my life to Sister Thérèse of the Child Jesus.

It was on March 14, 1916, on the eve of my second departure for the front, that one of my comrades gave me an image of the little saint, telling me: "They say she has already performed many miracles for the soldiers, and that she protects them." Until then, I didn't know her, but since that day, I have never stopped praying to her every night, saying in her honor the Our Father and the Hail Mary. Soon afterward, on April 30, I took part in the bloody battle of Le Mort-Homme,[1] near Verdun, and in the midst of a terrible struggle, while I was fighting, I called to Sister Thérèse. I invoked her, not out of fear, for I never was afraid, but I asked her to support my courage, for it was quite needed at that tragic moment! All of a sudden, in the clash, 20 meters away from the enemy, I received shrapnel right in my chest. I lost consciousness, and when I regained it, the battle was still raging. Worn out, losing my blood, I didn't have the strength to drag myself aside, but, remembering my holy Protector, I exclaimed: "Sister Thérèse of the Child Jesus, don't abandon me!" She heard my beseeching cry, for, under the spray of bullets, the stretcher bearers arrived almost immediately to pick me up and transported me to the first dressing post. There, a good chaplain, considering my condition was very serious, gave me last rites to the sound of the cannon. In spite of my pains, I was happy, and I thought with gratitude that I owed this religious assistance to Sister Thérèse. Dear little saint, I had so much confidence in her, that once sheltered from the bullets, I prayed her to grant me a second miracle: to heal my wound and lead me to her grave in Lisieux. And here we are, my prayer was heard, for thanks to her I recovered, and then I was transferred to another army corps and sent to Cherbourg. My first furlough is to come and thank her today.

[1] Le Mort-Homme ("Dead Man's Hill"), a hill located near Verdun, was the scene of repeated French and German attacks and counter-attacks in February 1916, resulting in heavy casualties on both sides.

How joyful and delighted my heart is! Kneeling at her grave, I beseeched her not to abandon me; it did me good to confess all my faults to her as I would have to a priest, she will have God forgive them. Now I feel ready for all sacrifices, for all sufferings, for the saint made me understand that this way I would expiate my sins and that anyway, Jesus Christ had endured for us more than all that. So that from now onwards, I want to climb to my own Calvary without a complaint.

Sister Thérèse of the Child Jesus, protect me always and help me!

Prisoner, that doesn't in any way appeal to me

Reverend Mother,

Having been favored recently in a very special way by your angelical Sister Thérèse of the Child Jesus, it was suggested to me that I should inform you about it, so as to contribute by that means to the cultus of Sister Thérèse, which I am now pleased to do. Soldier of the 174th Infantry Regiment, I had commended myself in a special way to your little saint and had already obtained favors from her, when on February 28, I received a more noteworthy one. We were in the vicinity of Verdun. We attacked at night, we went ahead in spite of the casualties; but at dawn: a difficult situation. What remained of my unit found itself 30 meters away from Germans in very large numbers, who summoned us to surrender and began to encircle us. After some discussion, with certain massacre in sight, everyone ended up agreeing to surrender and lay down our weapons and equipment. Being a prisoner—that didn't in any way appeal to me, on the contrary. So without a word I turned back with all that I had: backpack, rifle, etc.

I had to cross about 150 meters to reach a precarious shelter, the only one behind us. Three of my comrades did the same. First, everything went well, but the Boches soon saw us and shot at us. One of us was killed, another one was badly wounded, the third more lightly wounded, and lastly a bullet went through my thigh, without breaking anything.

I omitted to tell you that while I was turning back, knowing all the risks I was running, I recommended myself particularly to Sister Thérèse. I will not claim this was a miracle, since two of my comrades were also only wounded, and lightly so; nonetheless I see myself as the protégé of Sister Thérèse, for the fact remains that we all could have been killed three times before we reached the shelter that was behind us.

At the dressing post, we feared all day the Boches would burst in, but as it turned out, they didn't. I am presently in the hospital, my wound is well on the road to recovery, and it only remains for me to thank Sister Thérèse, which I do with all my heart. If the knowledge of these few facts could help to bring her glory, I would be delighted.

I beg to remain, Reverend Mother, your most respectful servant,

ANDRÉ RUOTTE

Don't be afraid, you will be saved

Coudekerque-Branche,[1] April 8, 1916

Reverend Mother,

You'll find hereby attached the sum of 50 francs, to keep a promise to Sister Thérèse of the Child Jesus, who saved my life in the following circumstances.

On Saturday, October 10, 1914, my company, the 10th Battalion of the 8th Territorial Regiment, was at the rear of the 3rd Battalion, which was going back to Lille.[2] Since this battalion soon left us behind to go forward more quickly, we were attacked by the German cavalry at the village of Radinghem, 9 kilometers away from Lille. Having neither cannon nor battery, and slaughtered by the enemy fire, we retreated to Armentières.

Being a sub-officer, I had the honor of being especially aimed at, and three machine guns were shooting at me. Without the assistance of this good Sister Thérèse, I should have been killed a thousand times. Nonetheless a bullet reached me, breaking the neck of my femur, and I fell into a ditch full of water, on the side of the road.

I expected to be discovered and taken prisoner, when, much to my surprise, after twenty minutes, good French farmers came to pick me up. They had hardly hidden me in their barn, with two horses, when German soldiers entered the farm and searched it thoroughly to discover

[1] A French town not far from the Belgian border.
[2] A city in northern France, occupied by the Germans from October 1914 to October 1918.

me, but it was in vain, and they left annoyed. I lived this way for a week at these good farmers' house, and in spite of searches performed up to ten times a day in order to find me, never did an enemy enter the place I had taken refuge. I was quite convinced that Sister Thérèse was guarding me, and I never failed to invoke her at each new attempt. I even seemed to see her before the door, defending the entrance. Once, for instance, my charitable hosts came in all haste to tell me: "It's all over! The Germans are here!" So I beseeched my powerful Protector to ward off this extreme danger, and all of a sudden I saw the following words written in white letters above the door: "Don't be afraid, you will be saved." Indeed, the soldiers visited the nearby barns and the yard but failed to find me. At last, thanks to the dear saint, after a week I was taken in by an English patrol.

When I remember the dangers run during this week, I can't find words expressive enough to show my gratitude. I am doing the impossible to spread her devotion, and all the friends or relatives to whom I gave out her images also acknowledge they are being protected. Reverend Mother, you can publish my report, so as to increase, if possible, the soldiers' confidence in the saint of Lisieux.

Your respectful servant,

MARCEL DUTOIT,
ex-sergeant,
8th Territorial Infantry Regiment,
10th Company, 3rd Battalion

Spiritual aesthetics

Madam,

I feel the need to tell you that, during this horrible war, I especially put my confidence in your sister Thérèse of the Child Jesus. My attention had been particularly drawn to her in the beginning of the year 1915, when my family and I were worried about one of my brothers, who was being very exposed at the Alsace front. Sadly it was too late: as we were informed a few days later, my brother had already been killed, on December 26, 1914, during violent fighting in Alsace.

This is when I beseeched the little Sister Thérèse of the Child Jesus to protect the rest of my family against the risks and consequences of this dreadful war. I went myself to the front, carrying on me a portrait and a relic of the "little saint," as tokens of protection and a happy return home.

More recently, during a conversation with a priest, I learnt there is some sort of pre-established harmony between the ideas of your little saint on *moral beauty, spiritual aesthetics*, and a big philosophical book I have in mind, which is the main work of my whole intellectual life, and of which I have published only first drafts: Sister Thérèse of the Child Jesus could be the best exemplification of one of this book's chapters, regarding the *life* of beauty and the moral beauty of action, and I propose to thus contribute to her intellectual glorification. Finally, the virtue of "providential abandonment," and of "spiritual assistance," which this little Saint so specially practiced, predestinated me, *by contrast*, to place myself under her special protection, for my soul, worn out by a series of tribulations, exhausted, weakened by a state of chronic distress, endlessly eaten away by spiritual anguish, does not know how to abandon itself like a child to God's paternal providence. My soul, which was already used to suffering and anguish, and to which the war brought additional anguishes, took refuge in the Little Thérèse, whose cheerful and amiable protection was well suited to this time of horror, and who took pleasure in "showering roses."[1] Hurt by so many thorns, dreading new, even more ghastly pangs from this war, I asked her for roses. And, on March 8, a day on which I had been particularly impressed by the fatal risks of the war, I made a vow to the Little Thérèse to go on a pilgrimage to Lisieux with my wife, and to bring there an offering of 100 francs, if I came back safe and sound from the war and recovered safe and sound my wife, my father and my mother, my sister and the brother I have left.

I feel, Madam, the need to write that to you, so that this letter would be like a jurisdictional writ of the obligation I have established with your little saint, my celestial creditor. Put it, please, in her former cell, so that it would be, so to speak, in her possession. I would be very happy to find it again when I go to Lisieux, and from now on, I am

---

[1] Saint Thérèse herself had predicted she would "shower roses," namely graces, after her death, and had associated rose leaves with her own devotion, hence the frequent allusions to roses in this correspondence.

pleased to thus form a relationship with the spiritual family of her whom I trust.

I beg to remain, Madam, your most obedient servant,

CH. BOUCAUD,
sergeant,
Divisional Head Quarter

Liaison officer

In the trenches, April 30, 1916

Here are two facts of extraordinary protection which occurred before Verdun, between Fort Douaumont[1] and Vaux.[2]

On March 7, at half past two in the afternoon, I was given an extremely urgent order to take to my captain. The 700 meters I had to cross were being furrowed with high caliber shells; to set off was to head for certain death. I must confess I couldn't help hesitating an instant, but recommending myself to Sister Thérèse, I soon rushed forward, now running breathlessly, now huddling or crawling. At last, I had the pleasure, half an hour later, to see my perilous mission accomplished. The little saint had guarded me.

On March 8, still as a liaison officer, I was handed over a cartridge pouch to be carried up to my lieutenant. On the way back, bullets were hissing around me; one of them reached me exactly in the area of the heart, piercing great coat, tunic, military booklet, and ended up ricocheting on a little medal of the dear Carmelite I have around my neck. The projectile went again through all my clothes, and snatched the suspender of my cartridge belt. The only impression I had is having been lashed round the chest,

---

[1] Fort Douaumont was one of the elements of the Verdun fortress, which played a key role in the French strategy during World War I.

[2] Fort Vaux was also one of the most important spots of the Battle of Verdun.

and that's all; I was not harmed in the least! The marks of the bullet's trajectory are still visible.

For these affairs, I earned my stripes of corporal, and a recommendation for being mentioned in dispatches, for it appears I behaved rather gallantly.

I am pleased to publish loud and clear these two events, which I call miracles. As for the powerful medal to which I owe my life, and the picture of the saint, they will never leave me.

JOYEROT,
corporal,
21st Infantry Regiment,
12th Company

Stolen bicycle

At the front, June 4th, 1916

Madam and Reverend Mother,

I've been campaigning for 21 months and have always had great confidence in the holy Sister Thérèse of the Child Jesus, to whom I have always recommended myself.

Until now, I had not been obliged to seek much assistance from her, but last month, being under heavy bombardment, I recommended myself in a special way and called for her protection. It was on May 5 in the afternoon; a big caliber shell fell on my dugout and smashed my rifle, which lay one meter away from me. I didn't receive the least wound, while the dugout was entirely destroyed. It is truly miraculous.

On May 21, I had stolen from me a bicycle belonging to officers, which I had to return at any cost.

I looked for it all evening, but I failed in my searches. I then recommended myself to Sister Thérèse, and on the following morning, my prayer was answered.

This is why, Reverend Mother, I am eager to tell you how much I trust Sister Thérèse of the Child Jesus.

I beg to remain, Most Reverend Mother, your most humble and obedient servant,

EMILE TUSSEAU

The saint of the Poilus

Most Reverend Mother,

Please allow a soldier at the front for more than a year to express, in his personal name and in the name of several of his comrades, a humble desire. We all are devoted to, protégés, favored ones of the Little Flower of Lisieux, whom we are pleased to call, in our warrior lingo: "the saint of the Poilu."

We have already been lavished with several of her favors, and as a token of gratitude toward our favorite saint, for our edification and the benefit of all our fellow soldiers, we would very much like to spread the fame of your so charming, so delightful, so good, so powerful Little Flower.

This is why, Most Reverend Mother, we would all be delighted if we could give out around us small pamphlets, images of all sorts, medals and other objects of piety related to the cultus of the Servant of God "Thérèse of the Child Jesus." In return for all that your kind heart will see fit to send me, I would love to offer some payment, but much to my regret, my very low income doesn't allow me to do so. I therefore appeal to your kindness, to your generosity, hoping you will condescend to hear our humble desires, as best you can.

I remain, Reverend Mother, your most grateful and obedient servant.

CASTAN

65

Tears

My dear Adèle,

I wrote to you only a few words this morning, quite hurriedly, to tell you that I have been protected, and am still wondering if it's true I'm still alive! My little Sister Thérèse really must have been much prayed to on my behalf, considering I've not passed on.

We are now billeted in a little village not far from the hell I came from and where I have left so many men of my section. I am the only officer who came back. When I arrived, I went out on my own to make an act of gratitude at the feet of the Blessed Virgin, and there I'll admit that I wept heavily. Oh my dear Adèle, it was so dreadful!

I wish I could forget quickly all that I saw; it is so appalling, I don't want to tell you about it in detail, it isn't necessary, I'll do it later, when I am with you and have recovered my composure.

Dear parents, I thought a lot of you during these horrible days, and it was very hard to know you were worried, while I couldn't inform you about myself. I sent you a postcard on Monday, I don't know if you received it.

Dear Adèle, I've just had to suppress tears again, reading all your letters that awaited me at the Company's post office. I understand your worries only too well; and ah, after these few days of ghastly life, to read again about your warm affection, which is so dear to me, that softened me; and then with the relaxation that occurred, tears came to my eyes.

Let us thank God together, together with the Blessed Virgin and Sister Thérèse, my dear Adèle, my dear parents, for we owe him many great graces.

I quite approve of you, my dear, my darling wife, for this trip to Lisieux you have promised to take; we will do it out of devotion. I have seen so many sad things, and too many comrades who were armed just as I was, and now have passed away. How willingly I acknowledge we must be grateful!

Today I'm quite tired, but not at all sick, and not a scratch. I assure you it is a miracle.

I will stop there for today, I will write to you again tomorrow. I hope we now have a few days' rest ahead, and also that our bit is done in this area. Anyway, as usual: everything is in the hands of God, may his holy will be done.

I kiss you all my dear little ones, and you my darling, and my dear parents, and your dear parents as well. How happy I am and how much I love you!

Tender kisses from me.

Your,

LOUIS

Dear Protector

In the Army, July 9, 1916

Dear Protector,

I have always resorted to you, and you have never abandoned me, even in the most critical times, and through your protection, I have already escaped safely four times from this horrible hell, each time with a mere wound.

This has increased my confidence in you more and more.

Here I am today, asking you to always grant me and my brothers your holy protection, as you did in the past, and to put an end to this horrible war, so as to bring me back to my dear wife as soon as possible.

I send you, dear Protector, my photograph attached to this letter.

While I keep praying, I ask you to always watch over us, and I await the end with confidence.

Your ever-faithful servant,

JULIEN EUDE,
sergeant,
119th Regiment

I'm gonna carry ya

Auxiliary hospital no 5,
Brest, July 14, 1916

Most of the men of my regiment, before we went off to the Somme Offensive,[1] had received images and relics of Sister Thérèse of the Child Jesus, so that we were filled with courage, and fully confident in her protection.

We remained several days under heavy bombardment, and we had only three wounded in my company. I was the first one to attack the advanced lines of the enemy, at the village of Barleux, on July 9. In this combat, very close to the German trench which my comrades seized, I received a bullet in my right foot and had to get back to the rear under a rain of shells. But before I could reach the dressing post I went through an hour of horrible anguish. 300 meters backwards, I saw not far from me a wounded man thrown 30 meters high in the air by a shell; and I found myself all alone, under horrible bombardment, unable now to move forward any longer.

I tried, however, by means of two sticks, to drag myself forward a few more meters, but I soon collapsed, worn out with fatigue. An enemy artillery barrage was raining fire on the plains; I thought I was lost, and I inwardly turned to Sister Thérèse. I cried with faith: "Sister Thérèse, don't

---

[1] The Battle of the Somme, also known as the Somme Offensive, involved British and French troops. It took place between July and November 1916 and was one of the bloodiest battles in human history.

abandon me! You can save me if you will!" Two minutes later, a Senegalese[2] was coming to me hurriedly: "I'm gonna carry ya," he said. Then, loading me over his shoulders, he carried me away at top speed to the French post; I was safe!

Thanks be to the angelic saint.

VICTOR LADRET,
28th Colonial Regiment,
23rd Company

---

[2] Senegal was at the time a French colony. Senegalese Fusiliers (who were not only from Senegal, but from all parts of French West Africa) fought on the Western Front, along with other colonial regiments.

The embodiment of goodness

July 20, 1916

Dear Sister Superior,

I send you these few words from the depths of a dugout located at the bank of Yser. I am a sergeant in the 123rd Territorial Regiment, and at the front since November 4, 1914. I am the father of a family, aged forty-two and a half. My wife, my son, and my daughter pray to God every day for the poor absent dad. I have gone through many dangers and up to this day the Good Lord has protected me. It is true that I belong to a very religious family. Two of my sisters are nuns: one is a prisoner in Belgium,[1] the other one is secularized in France.[2] Every day, prayers on my behalf are found in great numbers on the road to Heaven.

A comrade introduced me to the admirable life of Sister Thérèse of the Child Jesus. This holy and meek figure appeals to me so much that I feel disposed to trust her entirely. I would be so grateful to you, dear Sister Superior, if you could send me her photograph with a little relic, if only a thread of her holy habit, which I will venerate most respectfully and confidently. This saint appeals to

[1] Belgium, a neutral country, was illegally invaded by the German army in August 1914, and then occupied for the rest of the war.

[2] In 1901, an anticlerical law forced many religious congregations of active life into exile. Some teaching nuns, however, chose to remain faithful to their missions in France, and opted for secularization rather than opening new schools in neighboring countries.

me because she seems to me the embodiment of goodness, simplicity, filial confidence toward God: it seems to me that she must be fond of the souls who have recourse to her.

I feel stronger each time I invoke her and I find special sweetness in recommending myself to her.

I would also like to have a few short biographies, which I would be delighted to give out around me, so that the largest number of people may know her, love her, be edified, venerate her and contribute to her glorification.

Please allow me also, dear Sister Superior, to recommend myself to your charitable prayers and those of your precious community.

I thank you in advance and remain your most respectful servant,

L. MALAVAL,
sergeant,
123rd Territorial Regiment,
11th Company

Don't lose confidence

August 11, 1916

The day of August 15 was very hard: I had a foreboding of hardship and said to Sister Thérèse: "I agree to be wounded, to lose an arm or a leg, but please, keep me alive." After that I was reassured. I fought ardently; unable to keep quiet in the trench, I climbed over the parapet, where I received Boche grenades; I received five, which I could throw back just in time for them to burst on their side, but the sixth one exploded in my hand, tearing apart three fingers and additionally wounding my head. I fell backwards unconscious in the trench, which the Germans seized, treading on me. This is when, regaining my consciousness, I felt a very gentle breath caress my face, and at the same time I heard a voice whispering to me: "Courage, don't lose confidence," then, all of a sudden, I found myself transported from the enemy trench into a ravine, where our stretcher bearers picked me up.

I testify it was Sister Thérèse who rescued me. To her, I owe my life, and I will always be grateful to her for it.

T.,
*honored with the Military Medal
and the Croix de Guerre*[1]

---

[1] Croix de Guerre: a French military decoration, created in 1915, rewarding heroic deeds in combat.

73

Over here, Sister Thérèse!

At the front, September 10, 1916

My regiment, the ...th Infantry, was stationed before Verdun, where it was to go four times to the front line.

On Thursday, May 22, Corpus Christi day, when we also took Fort Souville,[1] the German artillery was firing heavily. In this pressing danger, I invoked Sister Thérèse of the Child Jesus, in whom I have absolute confidence, and her action was really miraculous when I received the order to go down again to Verdun alone, to bring back the food supplies at night.

So I got on my bicycle, jumping across the holes and the rubble made by the bombardment. I reached the road, but this spot was the most terrible passage, since one can be most easily spotted. I was soon surrounded by a hail of bullets, so that I felt I was lost; I was in an ocean of iron and fire. So in my distress, I cried out with absolute faith: "Over here, Sister Thérèse!" No sooner had I uttered these words than the saint suddenly appeared to me, bright and with a large halo. With her mighty hand, she abruptly stopped the enemy's shooting, and not a single shell was released any longer, until I arrived in Verdun.

I gladly publish this extraordinary fact, to the glory of Sister Thérèse. The gratitude I feel toward her is unlimited.

C. DE B.,
cyclist, ...th Infantry Regiment

[1] Fort Souville: one of the major forts surrounding Verdun.

I have come here to protect you

Abbeville,[1] September 14, 1916

Reverend Mother,

I am delighted to give you a few details about the graces I owe to Sister Thérèse of the Child Jesus.

Since the beginning of the war, I have carried with me, with the utmost respect, her precious relic, and it will never leave me. I have already had many bad moments, but my little saint was always there to save me.

Among all the dangers I incurred, the most noteworthy was the combat of July 30, and the following days. We were in the Somme at the time, assigned to reinforce the first-line troops. I was serving as a liaison officer, and we had to endure the most horrible of bombardments, for four long days, nonetheless successfully repelling enemy attacks.

One evening, on August 2, we were huddling, a full half-section of us, around a shack, which was being smashed to pieces under heavy gunfire. A friar belonging to the group was exhorting us to pray in this increasing danger, and my comrades were saying the rosary. As for me, while I was praying to the Blessed Virgin, I invoked Sister Thérèse, confidently calling on her for help. All of a sudden, around 11, while the battle was raging, I saw her standing at the foot of a machine gun that was there. She was looking at me and blessing us all. She then told me with a smile: "Don't be afraid, I have come to protect you."

---

[1] A town in northern France.

Deeply moved, I cried to my fellow soldiers: "I am seeing Sister Thérèse, she is here! We are safe!" And as a matter of fact, not one of us died, and we soon got out of this awful situation safe and sound.

This is why I love her so, my beautiful little saint! All my thoughts go to her!

PAUL-HENRY JOLY,
soldier,
229th Infantry Regiment

I saw a radiant brightness

September 17, 1916

Reverend Mother Prioress,

Before I can go to Lisieux and thank Sister Thérèse of the Child Jesus, I take the liberty of writing to you what she did for me.

Wounded on September 25 by an explosive bullet that passed a few millimeters away from my carotid artery, I lost consciousness. Having quickly regained it in searing pain, I recommended myself to Sister Thérèse and felt immediate relief, to such an extent that I could reach the dressing post on foot.

The hospital train dropped me off in Amiens,[1] the seriousness of my condition preventing any further transportation. Immediately admitted to the hospital, I began to suffer horribly again, and I invoked Sister Thérèse once more. How astonished I was when suddenly, during the night of October 8 to 9, I saw a radiant brightness, and a beautiful crown. At that very moment my sufferings stopped, and I began healing.

I beg you, Reverend Mother, to favorably receive this token of my heartfelt gratitude toward Sister Thérèse.

LOUIS PICARD,
stretcher-bearer,
129th Infantry Regiment,
2nd Battalion

---

[1] A town in northern France.

Surrounded by a delightful scent

Passe-Prest, Saint-Paul,[1]
October 12th, 1916

Most Reverend Mother,

I hereby send you the account of the protection granted by your dear Little Flower to the brother of one of our young nuns, a soldier in Italy.[2] The man thus favored relates the story himself to his sister:

"I am going to tell you, as simply as I can, what I owe to the 'little saint.' I had been in Udino[3] for some time as an automobilist. When we presented our automobile to be repaired, the commander enquired as to the cause of the breakdown; if the damages happened without the chauffeur being at fault, it's all right: it is repaired, and that's all there is to it. But if the chauffeur appears to be guilty, he exposes himself to very severe punishment. I found myself precisely in that case: the accident had happened to me when I was alone, so that it was impossible to have defense witnesses, and the officers were having none of it.

"I had resigned myself, and was awaiting my sentence, not gladly, of course, for I was going to be transferred to another regiment, probably to the infantry. So one particular evening, I was strolling in the country mournfully,

---

[1] A Dominican convent near Nice, on the French Riviera.

[2] Italy entered the war in 1915, on the side of the Allied Powers. It fought mainly against Austria-Hungary along its northern border. To be sent to the front meant, for an Italian soldier, particularly tough mountain warfare.

[3] A town in northern Italy, near the Austrian border.

brooding over gloomy thoughts, when I began to think, for a change, of the little book you had sent me in your last letter. To pass the time, I begin to read it while walking. But the book was hardly opened when I felt myself surrounded by a delightful scent. Surprised, I stopped, looked around me for the roses that were filling the air with such fragrance: nothing, not a flower around. A second time, I scanned the ground that surrounded me; the scent remained inexplicable. So I resumed my walk and my reading, but almost halfway through the book of the 'little saint,' I realized that supernatural scents are often a hint of her protection.

"So that explains it . . . and my painful preoccupations immediately vanished, a great calmness pervaded me. All throughout the following day, I thought about Little Thérèse and, once my work was done, I came back to the place of the celestial fragrance, to verify if any natural cause could explain it. I was compelled to admit to the wonder: the little saint, whose relic I faithfully carry with me, had favored me. Her intervention was complete: a few days later, an unforeseen circumstance allowed me to prove to my officers I wasn't responsible for the accident that had happened to my motorcar; I was saved!

"Since that event, I have enjoyed happy days; from now on, whatever happens to me, I know I have a Protector in Heaven, and I have no fear."

CILIBERTI MARIO,
Italy

How to write to Saint Thérèse?

Darmstadt,
October 17, 1916

Dear Sister,

How to write to Saint Thérèse? Letters from above don't arrive here below, since the aerial ways have been unsafe for a long time; that is why, kind Sister, your prisoner sergeant sends you his greetings through Lisieux, whence I asked for it to be forwarded to you.

The Carmel—yours—is really the antechamber of Paradise, and I look forward to going there and fulfilling my promise. I'm not complaining about this long waiting time, for many are suffering more than I am, and while France is far away, with the bed of lilies covering your grave, at least your assistance remains with me, dear friend, and you take care of me every single day God gives me.

Turn your mercy away from me, however, to lavish it on those who are still fighting, for those poor soldiers, your friends, are suffering astoundingly. Let their sufferings, the mere thought of which is unbearable, be lighter, and merit for them the grace of asking for their forgiveness.

Give to my loved ones, to all those waiting in their homes in the countryside, the strength of heart and the faith that support the soul, for the arm of God has stricken the world and you know that our trial will last long.

I have received your charming image too often not to pay you back; here I am, with two of my fellow soldiers whom your ever-reliable hand has led to me. The three of us will go to Lisieux if you hear us; what we are asking seems unfeasible but if the impossible had not been possible to you, I should have been dead long ago. We therefore fully rely on you, and know your help is coming soon.

May the Good Lord grant that the great sorrows and sufferings caused by this war should find through you an effective remedy. Keep showering your roses, more and more abundantly, upon your dear Carmel, and send my regards to your dear Mother Prioress and your dear sisters.

Let me express, forever, my utmost gratitude.

Your prisoner sergeant,

GUYOT

Go to church and receive the bread of the strong

At the front,
October 19, 1916

Reverend Mother,

Since I have been invoking Sister Thérèse of the Child Jesus, it seems to me I no longer live on earth, when my heart and my soul are filled with such joy. I no longer have the "blues" as I used to; on the contrary, I am granted courage to bear all the sorrows and sufferings that I am presently undergoing. The little saint helps me to carry my cross every day and to follow in the footsteps of Jesus, and when I have finished carrying my cross, the next cross comes without discouraging me.

This morning I was blessed enough to receive holy communion, and I want to tell you how it happened. Way before my comrades, I had gone to the field kitchen to fetch the "java," but it wasn't ready. So there I was, waiting while smoking my pipe. All of a sudden I heard a voice within me, telling me: "You have time, go to church and receive the bread of the strong." It was my little Sister Thérèse who was telling me that. So, faithfully listening to her, I put out my pipe and went to church. Soldier priests[1] were saying Mass there. I immediately asked if I could receive communion, and they answered that I could. So I asked God to forgive my faults, went to confession, received communion, etc. When I left the church, I felt stronger than I had when I had set off, and I thanked the little saint for sending her voice to me.

I commend to her my poor old mother, my wife, and my two little children. I'll end this letter now, for I have to go to my daily duties.

Yours faithfully,

THE LITTLE SOLDIER OF
Sister Thérèse of the Child Jesus

---

[1] No less than 23,000 French priests, seminarians, monks, and friars served in World War I, as official chaplains or stretcher bearers, but also as simple privates or officers fighting among their fellow soldiers, since the anticlerical French law subjected priests to military training and conscription. These soldier priests, in close contact with the men in the trenches, successfully acted as unofficial chaplains, as well as real soldiers. They were casually called *prêtres sac au dos* ("backpack priests").

Rats everywhere

216 Ferry Road,
Edinburgh, Scotland,
October 21, 1916
Convent of Mary Reparatrix

Reverend and very dear Mother,

The Peace of Jesus!

I would like to tell you a little miracle of your holy little Sister, and if you have the time, I would be so happy to hear from you the result of all our prayers of September, and if the cause[1] is progressing?

My brother (Captain Bigg-Wither), who is at the front, had a dugout that was full of rats that went everywhere, preventing him from sleeping and taking everything, even a lit candle, and so forth. I sent him some soil and an image of the Little Thérèse to be hung on the walls, and in the meantime, I prayed much to her for this intention. Before receiving my letter, he had been sent to another place, but a few days later, I received these words: "Thank you for your prayers. I am now in a place where there are even more rats; I've been here for four days, and have not been troubled a single time. There are still thousands of rats, but they don't enter my dugout, or at least they don't trouble me at all, though I sleep on the ground on a few sandbags."

---

[1] We don't know which cause she's referring to, possibly the canonization of St. Thérèse.

Give thanks to the Little Thérèse with me, won't you, and please say a little prayer for the conversion of my brother, who is a Protestant. I tell the story everywhere in her honor!

Would you kindly send your regards to your good and most reverend Mother Prioress and ask her prayers—I pray for her and for you every day—and I rely on your prayers, dear Mother.

Let us remain one in the holy Hearts of Jesus and Mary.

MARY OF ST. EDWARD

I regret that I have no more French stamps.
I hereby send three English ones.

Breton machine gunner

I have now spent ten days in the trenches, under horrible shelling, and I thank God for sparing my life. At night, while I was on duty beside my machine gun, I always said my rosary, and shells passed over me and burst with infernal noise without touching me. But it comes as no surprise, for Sister Thérèse is near me, and I assure you she is protecting me.

So I give out her medals and images to my comrades, and they are so happy that I won't be afraid of spending all the money I will earn to buy these precious souvenirs.

I have already suffered for our religion and have been abused because I go to Mass; but I offer up these blows for the salvation of France and to earn Heaven.

Sister Thérèse's humble Breton machine gunner,

JULES PROVOST

Providential assistance

Alsatian Front,
November 8, 1916

Reverend Mother,

You will receive at the same time as this letter my Croix de Guerre. It is a token of the gratitude I have owed to Sister Thérèse since the month of June.

In the beginning of that month, we found ourselves below Verdun,[1] having already gone through three attacks, including Vaux.[2] The affair had been harsh, and we were persuaded that we were done with this cursed place, where we nearly lost our lives. But, especially at war, man proposes, God disposes! This is how on June 16 we received the order to go back to the front line, ahead of the village of Fleury,[3] for some work to be done.

For some time, everything went well. But, on the night of the seventeenth to the eighteenth, all of a sudden a barrage of unprecedented violence was launched: 88, 150, 210,[4] the whole range was at work, and was getting closer. We felt the thrust of methodical explosions; the Germans

---

[1] The Verdun fortress is situated on headland, so that troops always found themselves "below" before attacking.

[2] Fort Vaux, near Verdun, was the scene of tough combat, leading to German victory in June 1916.

[3] Fleury-devant-Douaumont, a village in a strategic position near Verdun, was seized alternately by German and French troops between June and August 1916, until it was entirely destroyed by shells. Its empty streets are now the location of a war memorial.

[4] Various high-caliber German shells.

must have observed our position by day, and by their staggered, tight, precise shooting, one can imagine the relentless crushing that wants to scour everything and annihilate it.

Since I was not on the defense line, but only on fatigue duty, I commanded my men to withdraw to a nearby communication trench, a few hundred meters away in the rear. As for me, before I had enough time to reach it, I was surrounded by heavy fire. Shells were falling on the right, on the left, everywhere. I threw myself into a hole, but the burst of gunfire didn't cease, and the cold of death was running through my veins. All of a sudden, the thought of little Sister Thérèse, whose medal I always wear, revived me, and I promised to have a Mass said in Lisieux, if I got out of this bind. The barrage immediately moved away and stopped; I was saved! The coincidence was too striking not to admit it as providential assistance responding to my fervent prayer.

I gladly fulfill my promises.

Yours faithfully,

CH. BOUNEAU,
sub-officer,
245th Line Regiment,
20th Company

Look!

In the Champagne[1] trenches,
November 9, 1916

I could fill volumes, if I wanted to record all the protections I received from Sister Thérèse of the Child Jesus.

In the month of June 1915, being in the hospital of Aix-les-Bains,[2] after two novenas I had made to her to obtain news from my poor family left in occupied territory,[3] *I saw Sister Thérèse clad in white, quite for real; she showed me five letters, one after another, telling me: "Look."* She soon disappeared, and I looked for the letters, believing she had left them near me. As a matter of fact, it was at the first delivery, on the following morning, that I was given *the five letters the saint had announced to me.*

Here in the Somme, I saw Sister Thérèse again several times; I saw her mainly above us, following our troops, and the more I prayed to her, the closer she came, almost marching with us. Another time, during my sleep, she was watching over me in the dugout. I told that to comrades,

---

[1] Champagne: old French province in the northeast of the country, where the famous eponymous wine is produced; it was the scene of an important campaign in the beginning of 1915.

[2] A French town of the Savoie department, near the Swiss border.

[3] Several departments of northeastern France, as well as some parts of Belgium, were occupied by German troops for the whole duration of the war. This occupation meant starvation (since Germany itself was going through severe food shortage, due to Allied blockades), requisitions of all sorts, constant fear of abuses, and sometimes deportation for forced labor; hence the soldier's anguish over his "poor family."

not staunch believers, and succeeded in having several of them return to Mass; they are confident that the little Sister will protect them, if they do what I tell them and stay at my side.

Finally, thanks to Sister Thérèse, I have obtained the Croix de Guerre, and an excellent citation; I can never thank her enough for so many favors.

EUGÈNE CAILLEAUX,
stretcher-bearer,
33rd Infantry Regiment,
5th Company

The Little Flower's machine gun

To fulfill a vow made by my brother, a Benedictine monk, at the time of a very bad wound which nearly did me in in July of this year, I have to narrate the circumstances which made manifest to me the protection of Sister Thérèse of the Child Jesus.

In November 1914, having taken position for the first time before the enemy at Baulne, a village in Aisne, I recommended myself instinctively to the very gentle Protector of those who suffer. Her goodness had been revealed to me recently by one of my sisters, a Carmelite nun. I therefore christened my machine gun with the name of The Little Flower, and I wrote this name in full on its shield. Intrigued, my comrades wanted to know the motive of this strange appellation, but I preferred to wait until some event would uncover my secret. Well, a few days later, a bullet passing through the crenel hit me in the lip without harming me in any way; on the following day I escaped a projectile again; and it did not occur only in *my* favor but, many times, "The Little Flower" and its crew experienced wonderful protection. So that, quite surprised by these numerous protections, my officer entreated me one fine day to tell him what the name "Little Flower" meant. I read to him a few accounts of Sister Thérèse's miracles, and he exclaimed, deeply moved: "Ah! I understand now the protection that envelops us!" Thereafter, each time we had overcome serious peril, he wouldn't fail to whisper in my ear: "It's the Little Flower as usual!"

It would never end if I were to relate everything.

On July 3, 1916, I was moving along the trenches when a grenade, hitting the ground, exploded and caused me fourteen wounds, five of which should have been lethal. People rushed to my rescue, and, feeling badly hit, I made a final plea, from the bottom of my heart, to my dearly beloved saint: "Sister Thérèse, it's time for you to show you are watching over me!" And such invocations were my sole prayer for several days. Transported to the hospital by a motorized ambulance, I was operated on there the following day; I was in very serious condition, and when after four days the head physician declared I was out of danger, he hinted to me that "my case had been quite out of the ordinary!" In all that, as in the rest of my convalescence, I recognized Sister Thérèse's gentle hand, so that I offer her my Croix de Guerre and my military medal. While I was being given these honors, I was thinking to myself: "It's my little saint alone who has deserved them." May it now please God to place her on the altars[1] as soon as possible, while waiting for France to raise a national memorial to her who did so much for the defenders of their homeland.

HENRI SÉVELLEC,
machine-gunner corporal,
88th Territorial Regiment

---

[1] Saint Thérèse was beatified in 1923 and canonized in 1925.

Come on, my friend, forward!

At the front, January 5, 1917

Reverend Mother,

Before sending you the following account, I consulted several priests, and they all agree that this new testimony of Sister Thérèse of the Child Jesus's powerful goodness during the war might give glory to God.

At the time of mobilization, I was studying philosophy in the seminary of F. I was already fond of Sister Thérèse, to whom I owe my late vocation to the priesthood and who helped me overcome all the difficulties I faced answering this call. Her protection had also manifested itself in my favor during a disease I was afflicted with in 1914—and I wrote to you about it at the time. But what can I say about the constant solicitude she has displayed for me since I have set off for the front? I would not have delayed relating it, if it had not been for a wound in my right hand that prevented me from writing. Now that I have recovered, I do not wish to delay any longer.

In September 1915, at the Champagne attack (I was then a corporal stretcher-bearer), I was entrusted with picking up the wounded and transporting them to the regimental dressing post, located 500 meters in the rear.

On the days of the twenty-fifth and the twenty-sixth, I was constantly hard-pressed, and it was only the remembrance of the little Sister that kept me going. On the twenty-seventh, about five in the morning, after a horrible night during which a fierce attack had been going on, I headed to the first line, to check on the relief of the wounded, when, having reached a ridge battered from all sides by totally indescribable heavy shelling, I felt my courage failing me. I then heard a very distinct voice energetically say in my ear: "Come on, my friend, forward! There are souls to be saved over there... They are waiting for you!" I turned around in great surprise, and how moved I was, *when I saw the dear saint, beautiful and most radiant. She took my right hand and dragged me along with her.* Believing I was having a dream, I resisted and tried to close my eyes, but the mysterious call became more pressing, and I was compelled to obey it. I therefore rushed forward, led by the celestial vision, which nonetheless I did not dare look at, so strong was the supernatural impression. From this moment on, until the complete fulfilment of my mission, the enemies, who were seeing me perfectly, shot not a single time more, and I could reach my poor comrades, mortally wounded, lying there since the day before, devoid of assistance. The first one I approached was actually a devotee of the little saint of Lisieux. I was able to assist nine others, and, after encouraging them as best I could, I had the consolation of seeing them die with sentiments of perfect resignation.

My officers vouchsafed to reward what they considered an act of courage on my behalf, with a mention in the Order of the Army Corps. But you see, Reverend Mother, that Sister Thérèse alone deserves credit for it.

Her intervention in my favor was not even limited to that.

On June 25, 1916, my sergeant having been killed, I set forth with the head physician to replace him at an extremely dangerous post. In the evening, after a tiring day, we were warned that several men had fallen near the German lines and that it seemed impossible to go and pick them up.

At night, though, I left with fifteen stretcher-bearers, along with the surgeon major, for the place mentioned to us. Indeed, badly wounded wretches were waiting for us anxiously, and as soon as we had dressed their wounds, we had them transported to the rear.

We had just finished and were about to go back to the main dressing post when several of us were mowed down under a real shower of iron and fire. I soon could no longer see my way. Where to go? There were Germans everywhere! I was surrounded only by corpses, torn apart anew by shells. So, taking my crucifix, I pressed it on my heart and prepared myself for inevitable death. At this moment of anguish, however, Sister Thérèse's relic came to be placed into my hands all by itself, to remind me of the unforgettable grace of September 27. I immediately asked my way of this Angel of Heaven, and behold, I again felt that my hand was being held and I was being dragged along... I looked around me. Nobody! So I exclaimed: "It is you, Sister Thérèse, oh! protect us!" Then, without fear, I ran across the perilous zone and arrived full of joy at the main post. Only there did my guiding angel, my powerful advocate, appear. She was picking petals off a bright red rose; but I was not the only one who saw her: a comrade by my side was also gazing at her, and a few minutes later, mortally hit, he expired blessing God...

A sweet fragrance of rose immediately spread around us, which two soldiers pointed out to me with surprise and which lasted several days.

Finally, Reverend Mother, when, last September, I received a bad wound in that very right hand the saint had held, she deigned to support my courage during long hours of suffering on the battlefield.

There you have it, Reverend Mother, in all simplicity, the sincere relation of the very special graces I received from Sister Thérèse of the Child Jesus. If you consider it useful to procure her glory, feel free to publish them.

Yours faithfully,

H.L.,
seminarian sergeant,
stretcher-bearer,
Infantry Regiment

Nothing to fear, everything to hope for

Most Reverend Mother,

Through this modest card, we the undersigned wish to pay a tribute of thanksgiving to Sister Thérèse of the Child Jesus and the Holy Face. United by our convictions, we asked Sister Thérèse for the grace never to be separated from each other. Three reorganizations have already taken place, and each time, while our comrades have been scattered, we have remained gathered at the same billet. Every day, particular graces show us her protection and strengthen our confidence, which only increases.

We firmly believe and hope, convinced that, protected by Sister Thérèse, we have *nothing* to fear, and *everything* to hope for.

In this spirit, the inhabitants of the billet "Sister Thérèse" want, by appending their signatures below, to demonstrate their gratitude and faith to her.

---

[1] A French department in Lorraine; one of its main cities is Verdun.

Now, by whom are we protected?

In the Army,
February 7, 1917

I want to fulfil a duty of gratitude and at the same time meet a need of my heart, by proclaiming what Sister Thérèse did for me during the twelve days I spent in the terrible sector of V.

I had fervently entrusted to the little saint the guard of myself and of the young people dependent on me; we have obviously been protected.

On December 24, a relief day, we were accompanied, over more than 6 kilometers, by intense bombardment, the projectiles of which were crashing down all around us; although advancing on open ground, we had not a single man dead, not a single man wounded. Before arriving in the trenches, we had to cross a ravine constantly sprayed by enemy artillery; the troops preceding us had had bloody losses to lament. During all the time my section was crossing this extremely dangerous zone, the bombardment stopped abruptly. This astounding silence was noticed by many.

We remained five days on the front line, and while the nearby sections were being seriously put to the test, mine did not have to report the slightest wound.

As for me, I was protected from death by Sister Thérèse, whom I unceasingly invoked. An enormous piece of shrapnel came crashing down violently on my helmet. As a result I was stunned, but felt no pain, and yet, in the opinion of my officers who could observe the hole in my helmet, I should have been killed right away. I could offer countless examples; suffice it to say that, during all our stay in this sector, none of my men got the slightest scratch, while around us losses were quite heavy. But my good soldiers couldn't help exclaiming: "Now, by whom are we protected?" I showed them the sweet image that never leaves me, and the most skeptical ones bowed respectfully before this French virgin, who promised to "spend her heaven doing good on earth."

A. RITEAU,
sergeant,
413th Infantry Regiment

I chat with her

Eastern front,[1] March 23, 1917

I am a humble sergeant, of the class of 1914, at the front for twenty-seven months, and in the East for three months.

One day, in the Vosges,[2] a good lady showed me the memento of Sister Thérèse of the Child Jesus. "Do you see this little saint?" she told me; "she has protected many a soldier." I kept this remembrance in my heart, and I then chanced upon a prayer book here, with no name of author. I caught a glimpse of an image of Sister Thérèse. I then tried to remember what the lady had told me and began to pray to this saint and put myself under her protection. Since that day, she has never left me. I chat with her as if I could see her in front of me; she has protected me when I was attacking. Well, I always perceive her presence by my side, as another guardian angel. In this remote East, however, at the mercy of diseases and of the dangers of fighting, far from any affection, how happy you feel under the protective wing of a little sister you love so much! Even when I am no longer a soldier, I don't want to part with her. As soon as the war is over, I will give her my Croix de Guerre.

LÉON CELLIER, *sergeant*
157th Mountain Infantry Regiment,[3] 2nd Company

[1] Though the French army fought mainly on the Western Front during World War I, a few units were sent to the theater of the Romanian Campaign, on the Eastern front.

[2] A French department, part of Lorraine.

[3] *Chasseurs Alpins*, French mountain-warfare troops.

A Tonkinese

In the Army, May 12, 1917

Dear Mother,

I am a Catholic Tonkinese,[1] with the grade of sergeant. I am very fond of Sister Thérèse of the Child Jesus and know that she is always with me, for she has protected me well. One day when I was in the trench, a shell burst right over my head on the parapet and, through the power of this virgin, it didn't harm me.

This is why, dear Mother, I ask your urgent prayers that your servant Nguyên-Van-Giam would be saved by the little saint forever.

NGUYÊN-VAN-GIAM,
sergeant,
123 H, 3rd Company,
7th Indochinese Regiment

[1] From Tonkin, former name of northern Vietnam, a French colony at the time.

The most invulnerable of shields

Sergeant Maurice Jumel, of the 82nd Infantry Regiment's Cannon Company, is pleased and honored to communicate to the Reverend Superior of the Carmel of Lisieux the graces attributed to Sister Thérèse of the Child Jesus, during his stay on the Verdun Bridge in November 1916, and in Champagne at the last April offensive.

The shower of roses of the little sister Thérèse is the most invulnerable of shields against Boche shelling and all the other dangers of this life.

Yours faithfully and respectfully,

MAURICE JUMEL,
Sector 9

My Little One,
I have to get out of this fix!

In the Army, May 25, 1917

I write this letter for the greater glory of all Carmel, in the person of Sister Thérèse of the Child Jesus. A mere sergeant in the 70th Infantry, I have always had endless devotion and confidence in her.

We attacked this past April 30, and the fighting was extremely tough. I had placed myself under the protection of the saint, but the German machine guns were mowing us down mercilessly. At that critical moment, I said to Sister Thérèse: "My little one, I have to get out of this fix! It's for you to assist me, and I will report your intervention."

No sooner had I uttered that prayer than I was sent to give an order to the lieutenant, and, after a few steps, I heard a detonation behind me. I thought I was wounded, nonetheless I moved on. When evening came and we could at last put down our backpacks, I opened mine, and much to my surprise, I saw my linen in shreds, my sardine cans unsoldered, my papers and letters pulverized. I had received an explosive bullet in my back, which fortunately enough had stopped in time, not even going through my greatcoat. So I owed my life to my holy Protector. I placed my men under her guard, and she unquestionably watches over them.

P. BOSCHET,
sergeant,
70th Infantry Regiment,
11th Company

103

I am unpetalling a rose

Reverend Mother,

After suffering much, I found a position at the front that allows me to get some rest…

Here, flowers are offered to me; in memory of Sister Thérèse, I am unpetalling a rose, and I am sending you a few petals. Please, kindly receive them as a token of my gratitude for all the good you did to everyone, especially soldiers, when you revealed to them the Little Queen,[1] consoler and supporter in trials.

I remain, Reverend Mother, your faithful servant in Christ.

H. BROUQUIER,
telephone operator,
Infantry Headquarters,
sector no. 222

[1] Saint Thérèse herself, thus nicknamed by her own father.

Under Sister Thérèse's care

June 24, 1917

I am presently in the trenches of Alsace, on this ground for which we have been fighting for nearly three years! I have ample time to think about my little sister Thérèse in our hours of boredom; so, I comfort myself talking to her, and I experience deep down a peace of mind, a joy I can't explain. The war is going on and on, it's very tough, and when I think of my spouse left home alone with my little daughter, I turn back to the little sister and I find by her side all the courage I need to bear the trial; I should even say that a certain very intimate happiness is twice as big here as it is at home, *for my wife and I offer this painful sacrifice of separation to speed up the happy day when our beloved saint will be beatified.*

I actually owe to her a tribute of gratitude for miraculously saving me on July 14, 1916. I will never forget this day when, entrusted with some work on the front line, almost in broad daylight, I received an explosive bullet in my cartridge belt, the contents of which were instantly pulverized, and part of my great coat was reduced to shreds, while I didn't even get a scratch. I had placed this mission under Sister Thérèse's care, and while I was fulfilling it, I kept invoking her, and she was good enough to hear me. Since that day, I have never found myself without her, and I love her so!

EMILE JUTARD,
sergeant,
21st Colonial Regiment, 3rd Company

Mutilated image

For the greater glory of God and of his servant Sister Thérèse of the Child Jesus.

Reverend Mother,

It is for me a duty of gratitude to inform you of the miraculous way I was protected from an enemy shell. Soldier of the class of 1916 in the 41st Infantry, I found myself on Mont-Haut, near Moronvilliers,[2] this past April 20. There was heavy shelling going on. The same shell killed six of my comrades and wounded eight of them; I was among the wounded.

Slightly injured in the hands, I went to assist one of my fellow soldiers, who had collapsed by my side, mortally hit! It was only when I had arrived in the hospital of Bar-le-Duc[3] that I realized the extent to which I had been exposed, and also protected!

I was carrying on my heart, in the inside pocket of my tunic, two images: one of the Sacred Heart, the other one of Sister Thérèse, there was shrapnel there as well!

My great coat, tunic, and notebook had been passed through, only my shirt and the light cloth of the pocket

[1] A village in French Brittany.

[2] The Moronvilliers massif was the strategic goal of the Third Champagne Offensive in April–May 1917, also named "Battle of the Hills." The Mont-Haut was one of the coveted ridges.

[3] A town of Meuse.

had not been touched, one more millimeter and the shrapnel would have been lethal.

As evidence of my assertion, I hereby include the precious mutilated image and wholeheartedly beg you to have a thanksgiving Mass celebrated. Thanks be to God and Sister Thérèse, to whose intercession I believe I owe my life.

I am enjoying a one-month convalescence, since my right hand was hit, and I have the privilege of spending these few days with my family.

Reverend Mother, I give you all permissions to publish my letter as you see fit for the glory of God and the beatification of his servant Sister Thérèse of the Child Jesus and the Holy Face.

Reverend Mother, you can use at your convenience the sum that remains after the Mass is paid for. Reverend Mother, before I go back to the front, I greatly wish to have a little relic, if you still have a few ones at your disposal.

I am, Reverend Mother, your most humble and grateful servant,

BIHAN-PONVEC GOULVEN,
Ty-Méan Saint-Frégant (Finistère)

The protégé of Sister Thérèse

Roger Lefebvre, aged twenty-nine, roofer at Saint-Aubin-du-Thenney (Eure[1]), and family father, went to war in August 1914 and was enlisted in the 224th Infantry. He had unlimited confidence in Sister Thérèse of the Child Jesus, whom he began to invoke, he says, more than twenty times a day. In addition, he carried with him her relic and her image.

And here is the wonderful protection he was granted:

On September 17, 1914, at La Neuville near Reims,[2] about half past four in the afternoon, in a combat where shells were raining, he was wounded by six pieces of shrapnel from these projectiles, which cut several veins of his neck, wounded him in his head, in his face, in his thigh, and badly cut his foot. The poor man fell down and lost consciousness.

Coming to in the cool of the evening, he found himself bathed in his own blood, which kept flowing out of his wide open wounds, and feeling weak to the point of death, he exclaimed with ardent faith: "My Sister Thérèse, come to my rescue!" On the spot, he saw the little saint by his side, beautiful and compassionate; she was holding in one of her hands a big crucifix, and with the other hand,

---

[1] A French department in Normandy.

[2] An important town in Champagne. Its cathedral partly destroyed by bombardments was considered a tragic symbol of the horrors of the war.

holding with tenderness the right arm of the dying man, she picked him up, smiled to him and disappeared.

At this moment he will never forget, the soldier saw his condition change dramatically: suddenly his blood stopped flowing out, as if a celestial hand had dressed his wounds; then, no longer feeling the least pain, he *ran* to a dressing post that was situated 400 meters away from the battlefield.

Most remarkably, the whole time he stayed in the field hospital, his sufferings didn't come back, although the foot's horrible wound required operations endured without anesthesia.

Fully recovered, the happy soldier went to Lisieux with his wife on February 4, 1915, to thank Sister Thérèse at her grave, as he had vowed he would. From there, he went to the Carmel, and the Mother Prioress, accompanied by another nun, heard from his lips the heartfelt and uncomplicated account of the grace he had received. "I told everyone I could what happened to me," he said; "you see, my heart is still leaping within me when I think about it!"

"Will you go back to the front, since you have recovered?" the Mother Prioress asked; and the good private, carried away by enthusiasm, responded: "Oh! yes, Sister, I soon will, and I assure you I will do it without fear, for my Sister Thérèse, who protected me once, will protect me always."

The perfect good faith of private Lefebvre (who, by the way, is very esteemed by the parish priest of his village) was confirmed by several sensible persons. I will mention, among others, a venerable priest of the diocese of Angers,[3] Fr. Maurier, teacher at the day-school Saint-Maurille of this town, and His Lordship the Viscount Alfred de Rougé, who hosted several months in his hospital the "protégé of Sister Thérèse," as he always calls himself. His Lordship refers to him as a "fervent and staunch Christian, showing touching devotion to his holy Protector; besides, he is very intelligent and unable to have been the dupe of some delusion."

The rest of his story and his undying gratitude indisputably prove it. After coming back to his depot and now attached to the 24th Infantry, Roger Lefebvre was sent to the front again on December 15, 1915; on each of his furloughs, he made a point of going on a pilgrimage to Lisieux. He sums up himself, in a letter of August 26, 1917, how Sister Thérèse kept assisting him:

"I could observe many times," he wrote, "that I was being protected continually. In the month of May, 1916, I visited Sister Thérèse's grave, and, afraid only of being taken prisoner, I asked of her death rather than captivity. Nonetheless, I told her that if I couldn't escape that misfortune, I asked at least to be badly wounded, for I would have chances to be repatriated.

"On June 1 of the same year, the Germans having outflanked us in combat, we could do nothing but surrender; but I felt within me something that commanded me to resist, and I joined my captain along with three comrades. There, in spite of the summons of the enemy who wanted to force us to lay down our weapons, we fought back doggedly. After a minute, two of us were killed, and I received

---

[3] A town in western France.

a bullet in my right shoulder; but I still managed to throw two grenades with my left hand. I was then wounded again in my right side and my left shoulder and I fell on my back, unable to move. Very soon my last comrade also succumbed, as well as the captain, who was killed at point-blank range, unwilling to surrender. As for me, a German soldier aimed at me to kill me, but an officer stopped his arm. I remained like that three days long, lying down, unable to make any move, but in my trial, I could see that my holy Protector was not abandoning me. I was lying in a very narrow communication trench, and the enemy was advancing, gradually gaining ground; I saw hundreds of German soldiers thus marching in close formation. Well, not a single one tramped on me; on the contrary they all climbed the edge of the embankment at the risk of getting killed, so as not to touch me.

"Nonetheless I was completely exhausted and was suffering so much that I asked my little Sister Thérèse to rid me of my pains by sending me death. At the same moment, inexplicably so—for left to myself I couldn't make myself move at all and was getting weaker and weaker—I suddenly found myself standing on my feet in the trench and I could walk. I met Germans, and one of them gave me coffee to drink, rather than to another German wounded, who was annoyed with that; but seeing the gesture of the officer who gave me to drink, I clearly understood what he meant: he must have told him that I was more wounded than he was; as for him, he was given only water. I then was shown a dressing post and, as the bombardment of our artillery was going on relentlessly to regain the lost ground, and was reaching the post, a German military chaplain, with a gentleness that touched me greatly, helped me go down into a shell hole very close by. Eventually, I was directed toward the rear, to a hospital, for I was too wounded, and there I was operated on at once. I was afterwards transported to the Stuttgart hospital where I found good nuns who took very good care of me.

"I stayed in Germany until December 15, the day on which I was repatriated to Switzerland as one seriously wounded, although I had almost entirely recovered. This is where I got acquainted with private Latus, very ill with tuberculosis, and taught him to pray to Sister Thérèse. He listened to me and was healed at once, as he probably wrote to the Carmel.[4] I still couldn't use my right hand, however, since it lacked strength, and, as a consequence of an operation on this broken arm's elbow, abscesses kept forming on it; so I began novenas to Sister Thérèse, and at the end of the second novena, the abscesses had healed, and what's more, I could use my right hand freely. Since that day, I have suffered no more; I went back to France in

[4] [In the words of Roger Lefebvre:] In the month of March of this year, there also was another very ill soldier. I visited him and told him to ask for his recovery from my dear Protector. He assented, at which point I went back to the hotel. Once in my room, I prayed to my "little Thérèse" for my poor comrade, so that if he were not to recover, he should at least die happy. About ten minutes after my prayer, I smelled a scent of violets in my room, and couldn't understand where it was coming from: whom could it come from, but my dear little saint? On the following morning, I smelled this scent again in the staircase and had to stop, since it was so strong! About half an hour afterward, I heard that my comrade was dead, and I'm sure Sister Thérèse had wanted to announce to me that he was dying happy.

the month of July and was given back to my little family, overjoyed to see me again. There you have it, the most sincere report of what happened to me, thanks to Sister Thérèse. If it is considered useful to her glory, I permit that it would be published."

The protégé of Sister Thérèse,

ROGER LEFEBVRE,
soldier,
24th Infantry

Gas

I, the undersigned, Canon Henri Binet, military chaplain at the G.B.C., guarantee what follows.

On the first days of September 1917, I assisted private Ambert, of the —th Infantry Regiment, belonging to a Christian family from Marseille. He had been poisoned by gas, and his case looked very serious, considering the external and internal effects that were to be feared.

By himself, as soon as he arrived in the field hospital, the sick man expressed to me his desire to receive holy communion, and at the same time, blinded by the gases, he begged me on his own initiative to put under his pillow a relic-image of Sister Thérèse of the Child Jesus that he had in his possession, and he kept invoking the saint.

Nonetheless his condition kept getting worse, his whole face was but a suppurating scab, the respiratory system seemed deeply affected, and the fever remained very high. The surgeon major eventually pronounced him lost, and, as a matter of fact, several of his less affected comrades died.

I regularly visited the good young man, asking him if he still put his trust in Sister Thérèse, to whom I so much recommended him myself. Even when he seemed so absorbed that he was almost unconscious, he

---

[1] G.B.C.: *Groupe de Brancardiers de Corps* ("Army Corps Stretcher Bearers Group").

invariably reply: "Yes, I still put my trust in her!" And against all odds, the temperature decreased, external healing began, the body, become as a skeleton, assumed a more and more normal look, the eyes opened again, and bronchial congestion vanished. In brief, in the end of September, I left him fully convalescent.

H. Binet,
honorary canon,
voluntary chaplain

War dog

I got acquainted with Sister Thérèse of the Child Jesus thanks to a venerable chaplain who gave me her image. I took it with me to the front as a relic and experienced many times the protection she surrounded me with. Here is the most salient fact:

In the evening of Pentecost, on June 11, 1916, after a prayerful day, I was going back to my billet near Arras,[1] alone on the road, when I saw, by the light of the flare shells, a big dog who, after smelling me, abruptly rushed toward me, biting my left leg and not letting go of it, and trying to drag me along. Feeling lost, for I had no weapon, I confidently invoked the little sister Thérèse. The effect of my invocation was immediate. The hound loosened his mouth, and I could easily snatch myself away from its grip; it then ran away with a dull moan. From the way it had attacked, I inferred it was an enemy war dog, trained to chase French soldiers.

This bite temporarily took me away from the front, for I was sent to the Pasteur Institute[2] in Paris, and during my rabies treatment, my battery took heavy casualties in the Somme. I consider that a second protection; the third one was that when I returned from Paris, I was attached to

---

[1] A town in northern France.

[2] Louis Pasteur (1822–1895), famous French microbiologist, discoverer of the rabies vaccine. The Pasteur Institute was created in 1888 to support research on infectious diseases and training in microbiology.

a new depot, in Le Havre, which allowed me to go on the Lisieux pilgrimage four times. Let Sister Thérèse keep helping me, for she knows my desire to be the most devoted of her admirers!

CÔME CAMÉLIO,
12th Company,
3rd Field Artillery Regiment

Lost sheep

In the Army, November 6, 1917

To the Mother Superior of the Lisieux Carmelite Monastery

Pardon me, Mother, if I take the liberty of writing to you, but it was an error not to have done it sooner, to let you know the benefits obtained through the intercession of Sister Thérèse of the Child Jesus and the Holy Face, by means of a little book that was sent to me, containing the life of grace and piety of Sister Thérèse of the Child Jesus, and that never leaves me. Here is what I experienced and the favors I obtained at the battle of the Somme on September 12 and 14, 1916.

Shells were falling like rain, many of my comrades had fallen, killed not by bullets but by shells; at this moment, I remembered that I had with me the *Life* of Sister Thérèse, and that she had already worked many miracles. I turned to her in my prayer, requesting that she would preserve my life and that I could see my wife and children again. Yet I thought my final hour had come; but not at all, Sister Thérèse protected me from this horrible rain of shells, and yet the brim of my helmet was taken away and my greatcoat was ripped apart by shrapnel. But Sister Thérèse had heard my prayer and granted my wishes, and since that day my prayers go to her, to thank her for the favors she benevolently lavished on me. Yet I have to confess that before, I believed in nothing, or almost nothing, in a word I was a lost sheep; but since that day I have gone back to the fold and set out on a new path, the one Sister Thérèse has showed to me. Since that day, I have improved, I am another man; I should have gone down that route a long time ago, and yet my wife never missed a service and our two little daughters were raised as their mother, but as for me, I never attended Mass; and yet how many times my wife expressed the wish to take me there. Now, however, when I have the opportunity and we are in a location where it is possible to go to Mass, I don't fail to do so, and to say my prayers morning and evening to my protector Sister Thérèse of the Child Jesus.

Here, Mother, is my odyssey so far.

Please, Mother, excuse my writing and spelling.

Most Reverend Mother, this penitent remains your most obedient servant, may the Good Lord lavish his blessings on your holy house.

MR. HENRY GEORGES,
First March Battalion,
Regimental Transportation Corps,
postal sector 68

P.S.: I wrote these things to you to let you know Sister Thérèse worked two more miracles, saved my life and put me back on the right track, the latter of which is the most beautiful miracle, through which I can see the ideal life, which is a godly life.

Scalp

November 7, 1917

My good Superior,

I am writing to tell you that I was granted a little miracle at home by the dear Sister Thérèse. My wife was suffering from a scalp disease, and all remedies we tried proved ineffective... So on Sunday I got the good inspiration to put Sister Thérèse's relic on the head of my poor wife, and after three or four days the disease had disappeared entirely. What a sweet Protector is the little saint! I want to put a large portrait of her in my home, so that she may bless us always. I had the opportunity of giving her image to a good Annamite[1] soldier, a Catholic, and he sent it right away to his family. I was very proud to think that this way, Sister Thérèse would be known as far as Tonkin. I am the ever-faithful devotee of your little saint.

JULES PROVOST

---

[1] Annamite: from northern Vietnam.

I saw a sort of brightness

At the front, November 11, 1917

Sister Thérèse of the Child Jesus, pray for us!

In the month of June of the current year, I found myself at Vailly (Aisne), at the vast quarries named "Maison Rouge."[1] It was a sad position, for we were going through horrible shelling. Between June 9 and 12, one night when I was sleeping in our big dugout, I woke up and thought of invoking Sister Thérèse. Straight away, *I saw a sort of brightness, and the little Sister Thérèse who was looking at me with a smile. Oh, what kind eyes this saint had for me!* After a while, she vanished. I am sure that by showing herself to me, she wanted to encourage me and console me in advance on the great misfortune of my good mother's death. Going on furlough four days later, I arrived home, and she had already been buried. I will always keep a sweet memory of this vision, and, more confidently even than before, I recommend myself to my good little Sister.

E. T.,
16th Territorial Regiment,
9th Company

---

[1] The quarry of Maison Rouge ("Red House") was occupied by troops of several nationalities during the war.

I saw Sister Thérèse as an angel

Contrexéville,[1] December 23, 1917,
auxiliary hospital no 9, bed no 69

To His Reverence, the parish priest of
Contrexéville (Vosges)

Considering I have had faith in the Servant of God Thérèse of the Child Jesus since March, 1916, I want to relate the following fact, begging you to kindly forward it to the Carmelite monastery of Lisieux.

On October 3, 1917, my regiment, the 2nd March Regiment of the Tlemcen Fusiliers[2] (Algeria), was appointed to take possession of the sector of the woods of Caurières and Bezonvaux.[3]

On October 4, my group arrived in the valley, and I was appointed by my officer to defend the front of the communication trench which led to our lines and was situated 60 meters ahead toward the enemy lines, in case of an attack.

From that date to October 13, 1917, we were exposed on a daily basis to heavy bombardments and gas emissions, from which I was always spared.

There were frequent attacks from the enemy in the other groups of my regiment.

Seeing how things were going, I told my lieutenant: "I

---

[1] A French town in the department of Vosges.

[2] The Algerian Fusiliers were one of the many French colonial regiments involved in World War I.

[3] A French village in Eastern France, totally destroyed by bombardment in 1917.

expect us in all probability to be attacked this way before we are relieved."

And here is what happened:

On October 14, at about half past three in the morning, I was standing in my usual place, when I was suddenly dazzled by a great silver brightness, and much to my astonishment, before my eyes, I saw Sister Thérèse like an angel. She was walking left and right, holding in her hand a very short saber. I was compelled to follow her, and I found myself in front of a swamp that made a natural defense and was located behind our lines. I rubbed my eyes, pinched myself and said to myself: "You are not asleep, though. What does that all mean?" In brief, I went back to my previous place, and saw once more with surprise this vision moving about in like manner.

I then understood it was a warning from Heaven. I didn't lose a single minute; I quickly inspected my post and had the pins pulled out of my grenades, in case of an unforeseen attack.

When it was all over, I picked up my watch, which said that it was four o'clock, and I thought: it's just the time when the Boches usually launch an attack. I said nothing to my men, except that they had to watch well and be careful. I had been surveilling the side of the swamp for no more than two minutes when I saw a crawling shadow sneak away, then two, then three, in single file. I first believed the relief patrol was arriving and immediately challenged them in Arabic with the word Chkoune, which means: "Who goes there?" But the sole response I received was to hear a grenade burst, which, fortunately enough, landed beyond the small parapet of the communication trench. "Here are the Boches," I exclaimed. "Grenadiers, bombard!" I immediately threw three grenades; I then saw a German advancing toward me. No hesitation, I killed him right away with a shot of automatic pistol, and he fell down at my feet.

From that moment on, it turned into a huge exchange of grenades and almost hand-to-hand fighting. I didn't lose my courage, I stirred up my men, and, soon wounded myself, I only commanded the louder: "Bombard!" But there was no more reaction from the enemy. Down to my last ounce of strength, I sat on the parapet. Everything was quiet again; I was relieved by my section officer arriving with reinforcements, and then evacuated to the dressing post with all my men, including four wounded.

I didn't forget to immediately thank my Protector, who has always preserved me since December 1916, and whose celestial warning was our safety.

This declaration is certified by the author himself, whose signature below can be published; he recommends to all his comrades the utmost confidence in the Servant of God, Thérèse of the Child Jesus.

A. DIEZ,
sergeant,
2nd Fusilier March Regiment

We the undersigned of the S.D.G.[1]

In the Army, May 3, 1918
at the front, s. l. 132,[2]
6th Fusilier Regiment
in Tlemcen (Algeria)

We, the undersigned of the 194th S.D.G., having been subjected to a violent bombardment on the night of April 28 to 29, promised to express our gratitude in writing to Sister Thérèse of the Child Jesus if she would avert the certain danger that threatened us.. Our post was rather a shrapnel screen than an actual shelter against shelling, while a real rain of shells was falling around us. No way to escape, unless Heaven were to intervene on our behalf. The deluge of iron had been going on for three hours, when our shelter was violently shaken and threatened to bury us alive.

Fortunately enough, an invisible hand was watching over us; we are deeply convinced it was the hand of Sister Thérèse of the Child Jesus, in whom we had put our whole trust and our whole hope. She saved us miraculously; let her be thanked a thousand times!

In witness whereof we sign the current deed.

---

[1] It is not evident what this abbreviation refers to.
[2] S.l., *secteur de ligne*: "line sector."

Gothas and Big Bertha were acting up

In the Army, June 23, 1918

Dear Sister Aimée,

I want to thank you for the relic you gave me in the beginning of the war.

I went through difficult periods, but thanks to my confidence in the holy relic, I have always been protected, and I have good hope that the little sister Thérèse will not abandon me.

My wife wrote to me that I would please you if I could mention a particular fact: I'm quite willing to do so, for I really thought I wouldn't get out of it.

It was on March 24, 1918, when, as you are aware, Gothas and Big Bertha[1] were acting up. I was in the air force, in Le B. We had been warned there could be an alert during the night. I had a night off, I tried to keep awake as long as I could, but exhausted with fatigue, I fell asleep.

All of a sudden, an awful noise woke me up. I wanted to get up and see what was going on. Impossible—I was thrown back down, three times in a row. I took a look around me: not a comrade left. The bombs were having their way. I wanted to save myself, but where?... I burrowed under my greatcoat, pressing the relic and the image of the little Sister Thérèse on my heart, and telling her to protect me, for the sake of my little family.

Two hours later all was quiet again. I could stand on my

---

[1] Gothas: German bombers; Big Bertha: nickname for super-heavy German artillery.

feet, but what a sight!… Our airplanes all destroyed by bombs, ten men were missing. I rushed toward a wounded man who told me: "You are coming to my rescue, but don't you see you are in flames?" Indeed my greatcoat was ablaze, but I stayed safe and sound, getting away with no more than a little bit of the "jitters," for the bombs were causing casualties!…

Our bombers were destroyed! But the Boches will have their turn!

As for me, until the war is over, I hope the little Sister Thérèse will always protect me.

PIERRE BONIFASSE

The patron saint of soldiers

Reverend Mother,

I have the privilege of possessing the image of Sister Thérèse of the Child Jesus and the Holy Face, my comrades also have one; at the front we all consider Sister Thérèse to be the patron saint of soldiers, the protector of the front. As for me, when I take a cubby-hole, excuse the military term, or a dugout, to keep safe, my first thought is to display the image of my little saint at the entrance. We have no human respect here. I recently gave out images of Sister Thérèse to my company, but many men already had one. It would be difficult to tell you all the graces I have received from her, for they are many. This very night we will go to the first-line trenches, in full view of the Boches; please, tell your sisters to pray for us, so that the company comes back unscathed for the next meal.

I thank you in advance, Reverend Mother.

Yours respectfully,

MORIO

A prayer in the midst of the ocean

At the front, September 10, 1918

To the Reverend Superior of the Carmelite
Monastery of Lisieux

A humble soldier of the class of 1918 takes the liberty of
writing to you, to inform you that he has received graces
from Sister Thérèse of the Child Jesus for the second time.

I am a native of Reunion Island,[1] the only son of a
widow, who instilled in me sound religious principles
since my earliest childhood.

Aged 19, I was torn away from her affection and had to
leave my native land to serve France.

I embarked on the liner Yarra, and after a twenty-five-
day crossing, our ship was torpedoed[2] in a cowardly way
by a German submarine on the Mediterranean, on May
29, 1917.

I jumped overboard, in order not to be submerged with
the sinking ship, but swimming in that freezing water, I
soon felt my strength was failing me, and with anguish I
contemplated imminent death.

So, in my distress, I turned to Sister Thérèse; I quickly
said a little prayer to her in the midst of the ocean,
beseeching her to save my life. No sooner was this prayer

---

[1] A French overseas department in the Indian Ocean.
[2] Submarine warfare was carried out extensively by Germany during
the war, resulting in thousands of military as well as merchant ships torpedoed, which played a prominent role in the United States entering the
conflict.

over than, much to my delight, I caught sight of a small boat heading for me! I gathered all my energy to maintain myself on the surface of the water, and a few seconds later, was rescued by good sailors who had seen me drifting.

When I disembarked in Marseille,[3] I had only one thing in mind: to go to Mass and receive holy communion, to thank Sister Thérèse for interceding for me.

I can't say enough how much confidence I have in this great saint, my patron!

I remain, Sister Superior, your obedient servant.

MAURICE POTIER,
412th Line Infantry Regiment,
3rd Battalion, 10th Company

---

[3] An important French Mediterranean port town.

Gas gangrene

Most Reverend Mother,

With my heart full of gratitude, let me fulfill a commitment toward my protector Sister Thérèse of the Child Jesus and the Holy Face.

Badly wounded in my hip by shrapnel, I was treated in a field hospital at the front. Gas gangrene had infected the wound too, so that after four days, the doctors, noticing that I was too weak to endure a serious operation—the complete disarticulation of the hip—lost all hopes of rescuing me. My wife, informed, was to arrive only to attend my last moments: *science was abandoning me!*

When my wife arrived and was informed of the situation, she didn't lose her confidence; she pulled out of my wallet a little image of Sister Thérèse, the simplest one, which I had been carrying with me for three and a half years of war. She put this image, in which I had confidence, on my bedside's table. She then went to the poor little field chapel, and with the most devoted help of the military chaplain, she prayed and implored my protector. Four or five days later, without any surgery, the gangrene had disappeared: I was safe.

In addition, on several occasions during the war, Sister Thérèse protected me in a positive and effective way.

I remain, Most Reverend Mother, your humble servant,

ALFRED LEGRAND, *Engineering Captain*
Knight of the Legion of Honor, Croix de Guerre

Don't be afraid

Reverend Mother,

I am a humble Flemish soldier who can't write well, but I hereby send money to have a thanksgiving Mass said, for I am very indebted to Sister Thérèse of the Child Jesus. She helped me quite specially, and I am going to give you some details.

First of all, I assure you that I'm not superstitious. It was through a little book written about her that I got acquainted with Sister Thérèse of the Child Jesus. For a few months, I prayed to her every day, but then for some time I very often forgot to do so; you see, Reverend Mother, that I have not served her very faithfully. Nonetheless, I have always carried her image with me.

Well, here is what happened to me. On the night of September 28 to 29, when our victorious offensive began, I found myself on the attacking front, before the Houthulst wood.[1] There was a formidable preparation by our French artillery, and the Germans too were bombarding our lines. Waiting for the attack, I was sitting in the trench among my company, and I was afraid; then the bombardment caused me to fall half asleep. This is when all of a sudden I saw the little Sister Thérèse before me, just as she is on the image. She smiled at me and told me: "Don't be afraid!" I awoke on the spot, quite moved, and we had to go on the attack immediately; but I was no

---

[1] Scene of a battle in Belgium in 1918.

longer afraid and rushed forward with great confidence, thinking of the beautiful little saint who had smiled at me and had restored my courage. Oh! Reverend Mother, I have such a recollection of her apparition that I can still see her before me! I said nothing about it to my comrades, but when the signal for attacking was given, I told my brother, who was near me, to quickly invoke the little Saint Thérèse. Oh! I'm fond of my Protector, and I'm persuaded she will never leave me.

If you wish to relate the grace I received, Reverend Mother, you can mention my name, for what I told you is absolutely true, and I'm not ashamed of proclaiming my gratitude.

Please, kindly pray for me, and I thank you with all my heart.

Your soldier,

LÉON VAN HULLE,
Z. 160,[2] *10th Company*

---

[2] Z. probably stands for "zone."

She appeared to me

Contrexéville,
November 24, 1918

Reverend Mother,

Being immensely grateful toward the little Sister Thérèse of the Child Jesus, I am eager to inform you about it.

I have been in huge danger on the front many times since the beginning of the war, but the little saint has always protected me, and even appeared to me in several places; it was in the most perilous times and while I was thinking about her.

But the last time I saw her was on October 21, 1918, in Vandy, east of Vouziers.[1] It was about noon, we were sleeping in a dugout, when a shell came down on us, killing the two comrades by my side when it burst. Suddenly awake, and seeing my poor fellow soldiers lying dead near me, I was filled with great sorrow, and with fright too. So, as usual, I began to pray to the little Sister to have mercy on me, for I was without courage at the moment, and she appeared to me as she is on her image, but without telling me anything; I only felt she was protecting me, it was as if I read in her eyes: "I am here, do not fear anything."

I am forever grateful to the little Sister Thérèse, who has never stopped watching over me.

It would be very kind of you, Reverend Mother Superior, to send me a few images and souvenirs of Sister Thérèse, so that I can treasure them. As my regiment is

[1] A French village in Eastern France.

prone to many changes due to circumstances, you can send them to my home, in Le Havre, 75 rue de La Halle, where my wife will receive them and forward them to me.

Yours faithfully,

ERNEST CANU,
sapper,
S.H.R.,[2]
319th Infantry Regiment

---

[2] S.H.R., *Section Hors Rang* ("Reserve Section").

I lucked out with this fine resource

In the Army, December 12, 1918

Mother Superior,

I would be grateful if you could have a novena of Masses celebrated in honor of Sister Thérèse of the Child Jesus.

Since I have been mobilized, she has granted me such great graces that I feel attracted to her with unlimited confidence.

I have intimately associated Sister Thérèse with all my actions, and I am certainly very happy that I lucked out with this fine "resource," as a Poilu would say. I have never regretted it; on the contrary, she has always heard my poor prayers.

I read *An Unpetalled Rose*[1] I don't know how many times; I keep reading it over and over ardently. When I came across the precious book for the first time, I immediately understood I had discovered the saint I needed to protect me; I understood I had found a treasure. But I confess I must sometimes annoy Sister Thérèse, for I'm always on her heels: "Hey, Sister, over here! Hey, Sister, over there!"

If the devil tempts me, I call out: "Sister, where are you?" And I hear a voice replying to me inwardly: "But don't you see I'm here?"

---

[1] *Une rose effeuillée, Histoire d'une âme écrite par elle-même*: complete title of the first edition of *The Story of a Soul*, Saint Therese's famous autobiography.

Well, in my opinion she is a friend in Heaven to whom one can say everything quite freely.

After the war, I will ask her to bless my life, which I want to spend for the greater glory of God.

Yours faithfully,

A. L.
soldier

A poor sinner

Advanced Post Section,
January 14, 1919

Reverend Mother,

I have my heart set on thanking you personally for the prayers you kindly offered on my behalf to your little Sister Thérèse; ask her to keep protecting me and instill in me her love and confidence.

I have been a poor sinner until this day; I can't deny however that I perceptibly improved in doing good since the day I prayed Sister Thérèse of the Child Jesus to come to my assistance. Beside the spiritual graces, I also owe her the sweet joys of being back home, and of a union now sanctified by faith. I am just back from furlough, and my wife and I enjoyed the profound peace inspired by Christian love. We left each other calm, confident in the future and in God. "It seems to me that something supernatural has supported me until now," my dear companion wrote to me, "and though I deeply regret your departure, I didn't feel abandoned…"

How could I not be confounded by such powerful assistance received from above, from the dear Sister Thérèse particularly? I ask her to surround me with her friendly presence, in the ungodly environment in which I find myself, sometimes feeling so lonely!

I hope to go soon to Lisieux with my loved ones, and, waiting for this blessing, I remain, Reverend Mother, yours faithfully,

X.

Escape

Lourdes, March 20, 1919

Most Reverend Mother,

I have the honor of sending you a little report of the graces I received from Sister Thérèse of the Child Jesus. In the beginning of the war, on August 2, 1914, I didn't know her yet, I only got to know her over the course of the year 1915, through my wife—she gave me a medal, which I fixed to my watch chain and which I have proudly worn on my chest since that time. And since the day I placed myself under her protection, I have often implored her, especially during the battles of Verdun and of the Somme, and asked her to give me courage and to protect me.

On March 21, 1918, when the big German offensive was launched, I belonged to the 4th Zouaves[1] Regiment, and I prayed much to her, for the situation was critical. On March 25, the regiment was alerted, and we were soon engaged in the great battle. On the twenty-eighth, at 3:50 p.m., we received the order to attack the village of Boulogne-le Grasse (Oise),[2] and to stop the advance of the Germans, it was necessary to occupy said village. My company was in charge of seizing the left side. My section was to launch the attack. We started at 4 p.m. precisely, and I kept asking Sister Thérèse of the Child Jesus to protect me. Half an hour later, while I was crossing a road of the village, I fell down, badly wounded in my left arm by the

---

[1] Zouaves: light infantry colonial units.
[2] A French department in northern France.

bullet of a German machine gun that was very close to me. I had a big hemorrhage. One of my men came and dressed my wound, but my blood was still flowing out, and I began to be very weak. I crawled as best as I could to get off the middle of the street, where bullets kept coming from all sides. I remained lying during the whole battle in spite of all the efforts I was making to get up in order to return to our lines, and to avoid being taken prisoner. I asked Sister Thérèse for the strength to get up, and I promised her ten Masses, which were said forty days later by a mutilated priest at the grotto of Lourdes. I tried to get up several times, impossible, as if I were tied to the ground, and I had the impression that someone was by my side telling me to stay there. When the attack was over I got up effortlessly, but unfortunately my company had had to retreat, so that I found myself a prisoner of the Boches. But if I had gotten up during the battle as I intended to, I would have been wounded again, perhaps killed, so that I owe my being here presently to Sister Thérèse of the Child Jesus.

During my captivity, I implored her constantly, more than I ever had before, and I received many graces I can't explain, it would be way too long. As for my wound, I had a humerus fracture and a complete radial fracture in my left arm, so that the German doctors were about to amputate it. I refused. I was persuaded that my arm would heal a little. I presently have reached the point where, last Thursday, I began to practice again my profession of cook and served 150 dinners. I have a prosthesis that replaces my nerves, but still the healing went beyond all my expectations.

Back to the topic of my captivity, once I had nearly recovered, I was sent to the camp of Giessen, then to Darmstadt, and eventually to Skalmierchietz,[3] near the Polish border. On the first days of November, with four comrades, we planned to escape; the distance was quite long, though, we had to cross Russian Poland, Austria, and lastly Italy; with the protection of Sister Thérèse of the Child Jesus, we succeeded, with only few difficulties.

Consequently, as a token of gratitude for all the graces I have received, I send you my Croix de Guerre and a little red *fourragère*[4] my regiment has the honor of wearing: I promised it to her in 1917; please be so kind as to put it in the chapel, where I will come and see her again as soon as I can afford it. If you see fit, Reverend Mother, I authorize you to publish my tale in the book where the graces of Sister Thérèse of the Child Jesus are registered.[5]

Yours faithfully,

E. CAZAUBON,
ex-sergeant,
4th Zouave Regiment,
11th Company

[3] Giessen, Darmstadt, Skalmierchietz: three German towns. No less than ten million prisoners were taken during the war and sent to various camps.

[4] *Fourragère*: French military decoration awarded to entire units rather than to individuals.

[5] Ten volumes entitled *Pluie de roses* ("Shower of Roses"), published between 1907 and 1926, related countless miracles performed by Saint Thérèse.

Enveloped in a delightful fragrance

Plombières, April 14, 1919

Reverend Mother,

I want to pay a debt of gratitude toward Sister Thérèse, who surrounded me with visible protection during the war.

In 1915, I asked her one day to favor me with her scent, if I were to come back safe and sound. That very day, when I was thinking no more of this request, I was enveloped in a delightful fragrance. I wrote about it to a relative, and he smelled the same scent when he opened my letter.

The same year, in Alsace, during a bombardment, I received a piece of shrapnel in one of my legs. I picked it up when it was still hot and put it in my wallet. A few moments afterwards, I wanted to have a look at it, and from the open wallet escaped the usual sweet scent, as if the dear little Sister wanted to tell me to stay calm, that I was under her protection.

In 1916, in Verdun, I was knocked over at night by a lightless motorcar that stopped suddenly, not harming me in the least way, while I already felt like I was being smashed.

In the end, I spent the whole campaign unharmed, and as she had promised me, Saint Thérèse brought me back home safe and sound.

But I have something else to ask her, for during the war I lost almost all my family. My health leaves a lot to be desired, though the war rather strengthened me, and I am reduced to practicing a profession with uncertain prospects, since I don't know whether I will be able to earn a living or not.

This is why I can't send any offering for my good protector, though I hope I can soon make up for it, when she has answered my prayer again.

I am sure, Reverend Mother, that I will soon have a new favor of the Little Flower of Jesus to relate to you, and I remain your faithful servant.

PAUL APTEL,
ex-soldier,
359th Infantry Regiment

The free-thinker

V. (Seine), June 21, 1919

A little more than a year ago, I got acquainted with Sister Thérèse, the protector of the Poilus. A pious person had given me a medal of the little saint; but I was rather skeptical about "miraculous" saints, and, except for the Blessed Virgin, whom I have loved from childhood, I invoked very few of them in my short prayers. So I took this medal and mechanically attached it to my watch chain! A few days elapsed, and there soon occurred a problem at my work; I thought of my little medal and said inwardly: "Sister Thérèse, I'm aware you must not be very satisfied with a Poilu like me, yet I ask you to protect me. I'm presently worried about some little matter. Couldn't you attempt something for one of your new protégés?"

And the little Sister was good enough to listen to me, to answer my prayer and to grant me many other favors. That's why I am presently bringing my testimony in favor of the saint to be…, for she is a true saint, who does a lot for those who have suffered from the war.

Here is another proof of the attraction she exerts on the souls of the soldiers.

At an aviation camp I got acquainted with a corporal, a devil of a fellow, an atheist, but a goodhearted one, a vigorous and righteous man; he was a priest-hater, in spite of an early education that was basically religious. Yet he proved a true companion and a friend to me.

Now, one day, at the mess, over a tin cup of java, we were

chatting about this and that: our hardships, our future, etc. Out of the blue, opening his wallet, he pulled out of it a bit of paper soiled through contact with leather and told me while unfolding it: "Look, do you know what this is, you who are a 'bigot?'" And his blue eyes were gazing at me. "Absolutely," I replied, "it's Sister Thérèse!" I was astounded. "Well," he went on, "I will tell you that, free-thinker as I am, I still have a belief." And he confessed to me that he respectfully treasured this "reminder left by a friend dead on the field of honor."

I have no doubt that the dear saint will someday bring back to religious truth this man who unconsciously venerates her.

G. L.,
First Aviation Group,
3rd Company

I showed them the relic

Bugny, August 3, 1919

Most Reverend Mother,

I want to send you a detailed account that clearly shows how much I was protected by Sister Thérèse of the Child Jesus.

I, Joseph Bolle-Richard, from Bugny, district of Pontarlier (Doubs[1]), corporal in the 5th Artillery Regiment, 2nd Food Procurement Column, thanks to the powerful protection of the saint, miraculously escaped death.

In July 1918, I was in Billy-sur-Ourcq,[2] during the battle that took place near Villers-Cotterêts (Aisne). On July 30, I was directing the ammunition loading of four crates. The drivers were all busy with this work, when, all of a sudden, the horses, frightened by the bombardment, took off at a gallop. I envisioned a disaster: the men squeezed between the crates, one of them already dragged along, caught by his arm. There was not a second to lose. I rushed toward the leading horses and managed to control them for half a minute, which allowed time enough for rescuing my men. But I had to let go and fell down, trampled on by the horses. The entire convoy passed over me, that is, four crates, harnessed with six horses each, and weighing 1,500 kg each. I had five wheel marks on my body, and my clothes were torn off, ripped apart; I was dragged along 20 meters. Well, Most Reverend Mother, in

[1] A department in eastern France.
[2] A village in Aisne.

spite of that, I got up with no more harm than a light scratch in my face! A hundred men, who had rushed over to the place of the accident, exclaimed it was a miracle. My only response was to show them Sister Thérèse's relic, and they all agreed with me.

In truth, I have always trusted in this saint, and it was her protection that saved me.

Yours faithfully,

JOSEPH BOLLE-RICHARD,
demobilized since March 5, 1919,
farmer in Bugny (Doubs)

The hole where we were buried

Franciscan Friary, Paris,
August 31, 1919

Reverend Mother,

I want to fulfill the promise I made to you on the day of my pilgrimage to Lisieux.

During the war I belonged to the 62nd Artillery Regiment, 5th Battery. I had been fortunate enough to hear about Sister Thérèse of the Child Jesus, and when I went to the front, I commended myself to her and always carried her relic with me.

In particularly critical circumstances, at Fleury-devant-Douaumont, I invoked her unceasingly. Many of our men kicked the bucket; as for me I was redoubling my supplications to the good little saint, when, on March 14, 1916 (I will never forget this date), machine-gun fire was threatening us even more. So, with eight of my comrades, we had taken refuge in a shell hole, not far from our piece; we found ourselves on top of each other and so hemmed in that we could not even stand. The bombardment was redoubling in violence, everyone thought his final hour had come; as for me, I was praying to the Little Thérèse with all my heart. All of a sudden, a shell fell down near our shelter, and buried us all; my neighbor was split in half, as for me I got away with no more than a broken right shoulder. But, Reverend Mother Superior, the little saint I kept invoking with so much fervor didn't abandon me. First, *the hole in which we were buried became all bright, and I caught sight of Sister Thérèse surrounded by lit-*

tle children. Oh! How beautiful she was! And she was smiling to me and folding her hands as if to pray. Meanwhile, my comrades were busy unburying me. She thus kept watch over me as long as my rescue lasted, after which she vanished. I then asked myself what these children surrounding Sister Thérèse meant; she made me understand that it was a lesson, to teach me that we must trust God as much as little children do their father.

I recommend myself to your prayers, Reverend Mother, for on September 8, led by my great Protector, I will be admitted to the novitiate, where I will have only one thought: to emulate her virtues.

Yours faithfully,

LOUIS JULES

The blood stopped flowing out

Lisieux, September 15, 1919

In the first year of the war, I was wounded twice, and ultimately treated in the auxiliary hospital no. 30, in Tessé-la-Madeleine (Orne[1]).

This is where I got acquainted with Her Ladyship the Countess of Andigné, and after my return to the front, she sent me a relic of Sister Thérèse of the Child Jesus, recommending me to pray much to this saint, who worked wonders to help soldiers in distress. I was soon to experience it myself.

For a fortnight later, on September 26, while launching an attack on the enemy trenches, before Angres (Pas-de-Calais),[2] I was hit by shrapnel, which cut my right humeral artery, almost at shoulder height. Blood flowed out straightaway with appalling strength; it was like a spring with a squirt as large as the thumb; my eyes blacked out, I felt my ears ringing, and understood I was going to die. So, all alone on the battlefield, I exclaimed aloud: "Sister Thérèse, rescue me!" Instantly, the blood stopped flowing. There I was, stunned and filled with emotion, feeling better, though too weak yet to get up. A little later, I was given assistance, but they could do no more than basically bandage me on top of my greatcoat, and I remained with no more treatment until 2 in the morning.

[1] A department in Normandy.
[2] A department in northern France.

Nonetheless the hemorrhage didn't occur again. Picked up at last and taken by motorcar to the divisional casualty clearing station of Nœux-les-Mines,[3] I was there operated on to extract the shrapnel and ligature the artery. The head doctor showed extreme surprise, and after a sound dressing, he feared so much that the jolt of the car would cause a new accident that he forced me to wait two days before I was evacuated.

Sister Thérèse of the Child Jesus therefore saved my life, I will be forever grateful to her. This is why I am on this pilgrimage to her grave, to thank her for such a miracle on my behalf.

JOSEPH MARTIN,
sergeant,
149th Infantry Regiment,
6th Company

[3] A French town in Pas-de-Calais.

Waves as high as a house

La Coruña,[1]
March 17, 1926,[2] 11 p.m.

Dear Aunt and Dear Mother,

I'm hurriedly scribbling this brief note, I've just made a stopover here, for after starting from Rochefort[3] on the fourteenth in good weather, and everything going well until Cap Ortegal (in the northwest end of Spain), I was caught in a frightful tempest with my mainsail lowered. The ocean was raging, it was as high as mountains, and there was enough wind to bring down the ship's mast; I went to my wheelhouse yesterday at 9 p.m. and left it only four hours ago; so I remained there sixteen hours in a row. I really thought I was lost, for the sea was so rough that my ship was filling up through the wind tunnels and the smokestack; the beacons went off and I told myself every moment: "The swell will eventually submerge us, and it will be the end." I'm not exaggerating, these waves were as high as a house, and my poor little ship was completely disappearing under them. So I promised a novena to Sister Thérèse if she granted that we should escape it, and, taking advantage of a lull, I tacked and headed for dry land, to take shelter. I then went bravely on my way, without maps (they had been destroyed by the water), toward the

[1] A port town in western Spain.

[2] 1926 is probably a transcription error; given the content of the letter, 1916 seems more likely.

[3] A port town in southwestern France.

bay of La Coruña, still praying Sister Thérèse to guide me. Right at this moment, a Spanish liner was coming back; I signaled to him: "I need a pilot"; he answered: "Follow me," and there I was, entering with fanfare the bay of La Coruña, where I carefully moored my ship, good little Suzanne, who quite needed to rest. I then quickly put on my parade uniform, white gloves and saber, to pay a visit to the consul, and then to the Spanish governor, as the captain of a war ship and a representative of France. When I arrived, the fortress displayed its flag, I was received admirably, but I'm only authorized to spend twenty-four hours here, and I'm afraid I'll have to get ready for departure. As soon as I arrived, I cabled my position to the ministry of the Navy in Paris, informing it of my forced stopover, the safety of the ship depending on it. The consul then invited me to dinner and was extremely kind. I was exhausted, so he booked a hotel room for me at his own expense, seeing that I had been on my feet for twenty-six hours—but how many thanksgivings I owe to Sister Thérèse!

She rescued us and guided me as with her own hand on this difficult sea, which I had to navigate without a map, when I had never been there. So, have confidence! She will take us back to France and near you, once the campaign is over. If you could see in what state my poor little Suzanne is. It is heart-wrenching! Everything on board was upset by the flood, I had water on the quarterdeck at ankle level; our melinite shells, out of their compartment, bumped into each other from the rolling, and I expected an explosion before being submerged. My men were pale with dread, and one of them told me, as I pointed out to him that we had been saved by an obvious effect of Providence: "I too, now, believe in the perseverance of the Good Lord." I'm going to leave you, dear Aunt, dear Mother, to go and lie down, I am exhausted and will write to you again tomorrow. I embrace you with all my heart and I love you, asking you once more to thank Sister Thérèse with me.

I have just gotten up, and since I have a moment, I return to you quickly. I don't know yet if I will be told to go tonight, for the weather is still bad; I hope they will authorize me to stay here twenty-four hours more; otherwise I will go, and if the sea is too rough, I will take refuge in another harbor, for thanks to the consul, I was able to secure two excellent English maps of the coast; this way I will be able to take advantage of the least little creek to take shelter. My arrival here caused a sensation: people stare at me in the streets as if I were a strange bird, and, in my opinion, not in a very kind way. These Spanish races are more Boche than other Boches themselves...[4]

Back to my letter: here I am in Lisbon, where I arrived yesterday night, on March 20, to take refuge after weathering a new storm on open sea: horrible weather, the barometer at 742; the Suzanne was leaping under the swell like a bird, but the wave, as high as a house, was covering it from top to bottom; once again I recommended my

[4] To understand this allusion to alleged Spanish hostility, we must bear in mind that Spain remained neutral throughout the war, which apparently was enough to inspire diffidence in this patriotic French admiral.

ship to the little Sister, and headed straight to the little Berlengas archipelago,[5] between islands and dry land. I then made my way through the sea in a wonderful manner that astounded me. At last I arrived in sight of the Tagus estuary,[6] to which I headed directly; then having taken a pilot I moored again at the quay in Lisbon, from where I'm presently writing to you.

I'm back again for the rest of the story. I thought I could ask for twenty-four hours more in La Coruña when at five o'clock—that is just half an hour more than the first twenty-four hours—the governors' aide-de-camp came on board to tell me that if my repairs were not finished I would be authorized to stay until the following morning; but I found he had the weird look of a fraud, so that I sought advice from the consul. He told me to be on my guard, that the German consul, who was seen in a good light in La Coruña, was already demanding that we be detained. So I quickly went on board and had the anchor weighed without fanfare and went on my way alone without a pilot in the channel. It is true that I had the best pilot possible on board, in the person of Sister Thérèse, but outside, I found again the same tempest and had a hard time overtaking Finistère.[7] At last I succeeded; at the same time, I was sorry, for I had cast off so hurriedly I could not mail my letter, which I knew would have

[5] A Portuguese archipelago in the Atlantic Ocean.

[6] The Tagus is a Spanish and Portuguese river emptying into the Atlantic Ocean near Lisbon.

[7] A coastal department in French Brittany.

delighted you. As soon as I arrived here, I paid an official visit as a captain to the plenipotentiary minister, with saber and white gloves. I was very well received; I handed my dispatches for the minister of the Navy and the maritime prefect over to him; I then went to pay my official visits to the authorities, for instance the Portuguese admiral on board the Vasco de Gama. I was given military honors and all the usual fuss and am presently waiting aboard my ship for my visits to be returned. Since my engines have suffered damages, I think I will stay here three or four days, and will probably leave this coming Monday in the morning, so too soon for you to write me here.

No trace of submarines as yet, but we keep an eye open. I attach to this letter a photo of my pretty Suzanne, whom I love all the more because she has outrun so much danger. I led her into battle against the ocean, and she behaved so gallantly under my hand, that I love her even more now. I would never have achieved that without the little Sister Thérèse; she must have been prayed to a lot on my behalf, for without her we would be at the bottom of the ocean. There must have been several shipwrecks these last days actually, for at sea on one occasion I came across a whole set of masts floating, along with a large number of boards.

I will leave you now, because I must quickly mail another letter tonight. Until tomorrow! Many many kisses to you both, with all my heart. I love you.

EDOUARD DE LATOUR

A chance, a miracle

Dinan,[1] March 4, 1978

Dear Father,

1. I write you this letter urged by a very old feeling of gratitude toward Saint Thérèse of Lisieux.

I hesitated many years to put this testimony into words, thinking it was better to remain silent and not to consider my case an exceptional one.

And yet, today, at the age of 86, after a life strewn with great trials, I am practically alone, and have just been discharged from hospital after a very serious accident and six months of treatment. The death I brushed up against during this period has made me reflect and pray a lot in my bed.

2. I am an old veteran. 37 years of service, enlisted as a private in 1911. I climbed the ladder of all military ranks and ended up as a brigadier general, after attending Saint-Cyr.

From 1914 to 1918, I was badly wounded twice (Marne and Verdun), I then fought in Morocco, etc. But I vividly recall my Verdun wound (in Les Éparges),[2] of which I give an account below.

In 1914, in the hospital of Alençon[3] (after the Battle of the Marne) I got acquainted with friends of the Martin

---

[1] A town in French Brittany.

[2] The Battle of Les Éparges, a ridge near Verdun, took place from February to April 1915.

[3] A French town in Normandy (incidentally the birthplace of Saint Thérèse).

family, Sister Thérèse's family—they had me read *The Story of a Soul.* It must be said that in the army, we used to talk a lot of Sister Thérèse of the Child Jesus.

3. And *here is the main fact:*

On April 25, 1915 at 5 p.m., going over the top for a violent attack, we were caught in rough German heavy-artillery firing (205 shells).

After five minutes, three quarters of my soldiers had been wiped out. Nonetheless I kept attacking with the remaining men. This is when, entirely in despair, I was inspired to pray Sister Thérèse to help me.

At the same moment, I fell down, pierced by two bullets, one of which went right through my body!

Then the artillery fire stopped. I was lying inert and unconscious among the dead and the wounded.

At night… by chance, two stretcher-bearers noticed me and dragged me to a safe place… It really was miraculous (I am not exaggerating). I was evacuated to the rear, recovered after several months and went back to the front again.

Today, 63 years later, I am even more imbued with this extraordinary scene. Have never forgotten it. And as, in 1978, there are people who lose their Faith—or decide to lose it, I wonder if my testimony couldn't be added to others as a token of gratitude and thanksgiving to God. I apologize for this long letter, which you can use as you see fit.

Please accept this expression of my very devoted sentiments—thank you!

General JEAN JOUBERT DES OUCHES,
Commander of the Legion of Honor

As one whom his mother comforts, so I will comfort you;
you shall be comforted in Jerusalem.
You shall see, and your heart shall rejoice;
your bones shall flourish like the grass;
and the hand of the Lord shall be known to his servants.

ISAIAS 66:13–14
From the Epistle of the Mass
for St. Thérèse of Lisieux

TAKE THE BENEDICT & THÉRÈSE OPTION

Fr Dwight Longenecker's classic book explores
the lives and teachings of these two great saints.
Benedict offers the wisdom of age and
Thérèse the wisdom of innocence.

Made in the USA
Las Vegas, NV
23 July 2023